Deep Calls to Deep

By the same author

Reading with God 978-08264-6084-4

Deep Calls to Deep

Going further in prayer

David Foster OSB

Monk of Downside Abbey

continuum

Published by Continuum
The Tower Building, 11 York Road, London SE1 7NX
80 Maiden Lane, Suite 704, New York, NY 10038

www.continuumbooks.com

First published 2007

British Library Cataloguing-in-Publication Data
A catalogue record for this book is available from the British Library.

ISBN-13 978-08264-9774-1 (paperback)
ISBN-10 0-8264-9774-8 (paperback)

Typeset by Kenneth Burnley, Wirral, Cheshire
Printed and bound by MPG Books Ltd, Bodmin, Cornwall

Contents

Introduction: Godwardness

Many of us who try to take prayer seriously often feel we need a bit of help. It seems to be a common thing to feel a sense of difficulty, of disorientation and frustration about it, however good our habit of prayer actually is. It is easy to think we need to do something more, or get something right; that we want to try something new. I suspect this is often a mistake. The truth is often that a kind of shift is taking place. I tend to think of this as a move from 'prayers' to 'prayer'. It comes not from our inability to pray, however poor our attempts to pray seem to be, but from the fact that we have begun to discover something really important about prayer. What is going on at this point is likely to be disorientating because, putting it as simply as I can, what is happening is that God is taking prayer out of our hands and our job is to let him pray in us by the Holy Spirit he gives us in Christ. It is waking up to the contemplative dimension of prayer.

The title of this book comes from Ps. 42.7: 'Deep calls to deep in the voice of your mighty waters'. It gives an indication of what I think we are being invited to discover in prayer at this point, where we find ourselves being drawn to the depths of the divine mystery, which can sometimes seem a fathomless void, and where the journey we are embarked on is one that brings us into the obscurity and shadows of ourselves. The 'deep', then (Latin uses the word abyss), suggests mystery of the depths both of the human heart as well as of God. It is also the place of creation, where, in Genesis 1, the Spirit hovered over the waters of the deep, and in the Psalm the image expresses the correspondence between God and the human heart as well as the resonance between them. And yet creation echoes to God's voice, the voice of the mighty waterfalls, which sing of God's creativity and life. Nowhere does this happen more eloquently than in the abyss in our hearts, where God speaks and creates us anew in his image and likeness.

Much of what follows in this book is an attempt to make some sense, in a practical kind of way, of this move in personal prayer into a contemplative dimension. One of the points I want to emphasize is that at this stage it is less a question of our needing to know some new techniques about prayer than of making sense of what is going on when we pray. For it is a point where people who give themselves to prayer should try to do less and let God take the initiative instead. To understand this, I think, calls for a little more theology than is often found in such discussions – and more, I am afraid, than will actually be possible here. But underlying the argument I will be following in this book is the belief that prayer is not just a search for God as the ultimate reality towards whom we live. Christian prayer is also our response to the sense that we have already been found by God. And in this response we are expressing our relationship with Jesus Christ as a relationship uniting us with him and, in him, with all who believe in him. This new communion of life is brought about by the Holy Spirit, who draws us in Christ to a new awareness of God as our heavenly Father. In prayer, therefore, we come to share an experience of the Trinity, of that exchange of life and love between the Father, the Son and the Holy Spirit.

Introduction

Prayer is often described as a relationship with God, and so many of our ways of talking about it are shaped by a kind of picture of two people talking to each other, more or less 'hitting it off' in friendship, or (perhaps a more primitive understanding of prayer) as someone asking for something from an elder or better, or a child and his father or mother. There are other pictures we may have of this relationship with God. But I am afraid I find that all of them are fundamentally misleading and before long I think they can become a serious obstacle in prayer. The reason for this is that they all reduce God to someone to whom we can relate on a merely human level. They turn God into an image of ourselves. In the end we cannot pray to such a false God. As imaginative human beings we need images, but we also need to be able to move beyond them.

Basic to all these analogies is the idea of God as a kind of individual, someone 'over there' to whom I am speaking and who might be speaking to me. This idea also needs to be jettisoned. It is the fundamental mistake we make, which takes us straight to the difficulty I mentioned at the outset, which we meet sooner or later in prayer. While prayer expresses our sense of relationship to God, it is a very odd kind of relation. There is nothing like it because God is not like anything at all; and yet it is central to the mystery of our own existence, with all the ambiguities of human existence too: sharing not only the glory of being alive, but also profoundly compromised by the mystery of evil and sin. So without trying to analyse the relationship I find myself thinking about prayer in terms of a neologism, coined to name what cannot be described; I think of prayer as the exploration of our Godwardness. By 'Godwardness' I mean the way we see ourselves living from and towards him, seeking him, but aware also of being constantly in his presence.

Henri le Saux (1910–1973), the Benedictine monk who went to live in an Indian ashram and worked under the name Abhishiktananda, is said to have asked a group of children where God was for them. Half of them pointed up to the sky: he was 'up there'. Half pointed to their hearts: he was 'in there'. According to the story, the Christians all pointed upwards, while the Hindus all pointed inwards. But for both Christians and Hindus that would be an oversimplification: God is nowhere in the sense of being pointed at; or he is everywhere without being in any place. We just cannot put God anywhere in terms of place. But we have to use these kinds of ideas metaphorically because we need to express relationship in spatial terms, not because God is anywhere in particular. For me, 'God-wardness' catches the ambivalence of this sense of direction or orientation, both inwards and outwards.

Those of us for whom prayer is a high priority have begun to discover that that relationship, however it is to be understood, is so fundamental to who we are, what we are, and what we are about, that all these spatial metaphors are full of meaning. St Paul said 'In him we live and move and have our being' and sometimes we know exactly what that means. But Paul was speaking in an apologetic context to Athenians (Acts 17.22-28) in order to try to get a conversation about God going; sometimes we find ourselves relating more to the unknown God whose altar had so struck the apostle. In other words, our relationship to God and our dependence on him can be obvious to the eyes of faith; but we can also find ourselves stretching out to him, wondering if he is 'there' (in any appropriate sense at all), confronted by an eerie sense of distance, of absence, of difficulty in making sense of what we are trying to do in the first place, clutching as it seems at thin air. Prayer is a response to God's mysterious presence, but it is also a search, it springs from a sense of need of one whom we have yet to find, without whom our lives are incomplete.

The birth of contemplative prayer can reveal a different kind of difficulty as well. When we try to pray we can seem to fail to connect even with ourselves; we feel less the absence of God than our alienation from ourselves. A saint to whom I am myself particularly devoted, St Augustine of Hippo, has helped me make more sense of this experience than anyone else I have come across. In his conversion experience he describes a particularly vivid awareness of God's presence and reality, but it took him a long time to get there; 'late have I loved thee', as he put it in *Confessions* X.27.38.

These two factors, God's difference from the world, with the impossibility of getting very far in spelling out our relationship to him linguistically, and a human being's sense of inner alienation, underlie the difficulty of much of our talking about prayer, and the elusiveness of the concepts habitually used to do so. In particular there are three constellations of words that are frequently used in talking about prayer, and which seem to me to help in various ways to open up our interiority or, better, what I have been calling our Godwardness.

The elusiveness of God in human experience seems to me to underlie the complexity of much of the language used about the mind, and the possibility of knowing, seeing and paying attention to God, or understanding his will. The development of this language has been strongly influenced by early writers who were influenced by Platonism. It has not won universal approval, and some regard Platonism as an unwelcome intrusion. But one of the important legacies of this tradition is the way it has helped to talk about the way knowledge and understanding are more than the work of a discursive reason, and limited by the concepts we devise to talk about our experience. We know more than we can say, and the language of non-conceptual knowledge and insight stemming from this tradition has been a vital element in Christian thought about prayer.

Alongside this is another group of words associated with the heart. Here I think the language of prayer is trying to explore the way in which we seek to embrace what ultimately eludes our knowledge and are able to shape our lives accordingly, or be shaped by it. The biblical roots of this language mean that it is rather allusive in the terms of later, non-Semitic philosophical traditions, but it includes our loving, willing and desiring, our readiness to make commitments and our integrity in living them out faithfully.

Finally there is a constellation of psychological words, around 'soul' (*psyche* in Greek), 'spirit' and 'self', which are rather harder to place. In general 'soul' seems to me to observe some kind of distinction from body, and perhaps in principle to distinguish a living from a dead body. I think in terms of 'soul' in order to refer to my life as 'given' me by God. This is not really the way the philosophical tradition, in particular associated with the name of Descartes, has used the term; it is rather closer to what I understand the Hebrew idea of life or spirit to be. The idea of 'spirit', therefore, looks to the way we believe our lives to be dependent on God, and to belong to a world beyond the material and intellectual order; and in this context the ambiguity that sometimes occurs in our experience between 'spirit' as human and created and 'Spirit' as Holy and uncreated is true to the way the Bible sees our lives as breathed into us by God. Clearly the two must be distinguished metaphysically, but it has often proved hard to do so in practice.

Then there are more modern terms like 'self' and the words of identity such as 'ego' or 'person'. I will try to explain how I use them later on in Chapter Five. Their value is in the way they help us explore our subjectivity. For I can see myself externally in relationships to other people, and in relation to them as playing certain roles. This is how I develop a sense of my 'ego'. But there is also the way I stand towards God, and live out that relationship, which is fundamental to my identity in a completely different way. This is where I think the term 'self' comes in, obviously in a very different sense from the usual way we talk of 'myself' or of 'selfishness'. In theological language, 'person' and 'personal' also need to be understood in a metaphysical rather than a legal sense of having rights, especially rights of ownership, or the psychological meaning of 'personality'. Perhaps the simplest sense we need to give these words in theological use is to refer to our identity before God.

The kind of prayer I want to consider in this book is something we wake up to, something that dawns on us, perhaps, or something that shakes us more suddenly awake. But the metaphors of daybreak are also misleading. I wonder if it is not more often the case that it comes to us as nightfall, the loveliness of an afternoon beginning to pale inexorably into the darkness. Or just that we find ourselves swamped in the fog. This is because prayer in the sense we need to rediscover is simply our recognizing that our fundamental orientation is towards God. Initially, and for most people recurrently, this is a radically disorientating experience.

Reorientation towards God is to a great extent a process of learning that prayer is a gift rather than something we do or that we can produce from our own resources. It is often felt as something we can't do – but we know that feeling does not mean we should therefore stop. This is the paradoxical position we find ourselves in. Like faith itself, it is a way of knowing that unfolds by a process of unknowing; indeed, one way of thinking about prayer is as the 'inside' of our life of faith, its heartbeat and lungs, the gift of the Spirit that God breathes into the core of our being.

One thing that does help us pray is discovering how Jesus provides, in modern terms, the frame or model of Godwardness – and so of our prayer. Growing in prayer is a process of finding ourselves in Christ and it includes several aspects. First, and foremost, it includes our membership of the Church, which is the Body of Christ. But beyond that it includes our engagement with the whole mission of the Church, to spread the Gospel in our lives by word and deed. Our education for all this is found principally in our participation in the Church's liturgy. It is, I am sure, no accident that people who are really committed to prayer and to nourishing their faith in this way are more and more often people for whom the Eucharist, Eucharistic adoration, and the Divine Office or the daily Prayer of the Church are important elements of their Christian lives. In fact, prayer has what I think of as a Trinitarian shape, which is encapsulated in the words of the Doxology of the Eucharistic Prayer, when we turn to the Father as members of the Body of Christ, and pray 'through him, with him, and in him, in the unity of the Holy Spirit' that Christ pours into our hearts.

In Chapter One, I will say something rather generally about 'methods of prayer' but, as I have already said, the main interest will be in how they develop into, or perhaps better, disclose the contemplative character of prayer. Hence the shorthand phrase of a shift 'from prayers to prayer'. The key to this shift is learning that listening is in the end more important than saying. God matters far more than anything we have to say. The problem is that, unsurprisingly, listening is terribly hard. Some practical suggestions about how to deal with this are given in Chapters Two and Three. As we get used to listening we are able to put ourselves in the way of discovering the positive value of silence in prayer, which is the topic of Chapter Four.

In silence we learn that prayer is less about what we do than about what God is doing; it is something we receive. It engages us in the process of redemption and sanctification by which God brings us to glory, to our full stature as his children in Christ. Some of the ways in which this has been described are considered in Chapter Five, while Chapter Six considers the implications of this in greater depth.

For Christians there can never be anything private about prayer. Contemplative prayer is not just a thing between God and me – which is a selfish way of thinking about prayer. More accurately, what has often been called 'private prayer' should be thought of as personal prayer. Talking of 'personal prayer' also avoids the idea that praying on our own is basically different from praying with others, especially when we celebrate the liturgical prayer of the Church. It is not. Each helps us engage more completely in the other; they make sense only in relationship to each other.

Not only is prayer a way of discovering ourselves in relationship to God, as the way we grow to the fullness of human life; it is also something that includes our relationships to everyone else who makes us who we are. And, for Christians no one and nothing can ultimately be excluded from our concern. A deep commitment to prayer is a commitment to the redemption of the world, and means channelling the life we live in our union with Christ to everyone through our faithful living and our seeking God in all we do. In Chapter Six, therefore, a link is made between the inner personal process of forgiveness, healing and transformation and our vocation to be peacemakers and to promote redemption and transformation in human relationships generally. I talk of this as making peace.

Finally I will consider the way prayer is part of the priesthood of Christ, part of the way we stand before God on behalf of all creation. It includes not only our intercession for others, but also the offering we make of ourselves to God in Christ for the sake of others, which is supremely the case in our participation in offering the Eucharistic sacrifice.

The material contained in the chapters that follow draws on talks given at retreats and as Novice Master at Downside Abbey. Those familiar with the traditions of prayer characteristic of the English Benedictine Congregation will find, I hope, little original in it. To that extent it is a tribute to what I have learnt in the midst of my brethren and from other monks and nuns of the Congregation, and I would like to express my thanks to them. I would like to think this book may help open up to others the spiritual tradition of the English Congregation, not least its mastermind, the Welshman, Dom Augustine Baker. But I particularly want to express my debt to two of my brethren, now departed but who live in my warmest affection, Dom Illtyd Trethowan and Dom Daniel Rees. I pray they are now able to enjoy the uninhibited fullness of what we can only pray for in this life.

Routes
in prayer

1

I am sure we all learn to pray by talking, and probably we usually do so by asking God for things. This is not a bad lesson to learn. It is a good way to learn that God is there for us in that kind of way; that he is there for us personally, caring and supporting us in our needs. Whatever questions this kind of use of language raises later on about God, the way we relate to him, or our assumptions about answers to prayer, I think it is worth acknowledging this truth: we can talk to God. It is how we learn to relate to him, just as it is by talking that we learn to relate to our parents and then, gradually, to the rest of the world. The way we connect with others goes far beyond what we put into words but language is the way we learn to own that relationship, and make it consciously part of our lives. God is different, of course, from human beings, but as far as we are concerned it is only by learning to talk to him in prayer that we will ever learn to connect with him and to make sense of that difference.

What I want to explore in this chapter is the development in the way we naturally pray, a development which moves away from words to something rather deeper. Not that we necessarily stop using words, but the way we use them changes, and we begin to communicate with God in a different kind of way. I often find myself thinking of this development as a movement from 'prayers' to prayer. I do not for a moment think that this simpler kind of 'prayer' is better than 'prayers', but I do think that it helps us when we pray to remember that this kind of development happens, and that it is usually more helpful to follow the direction of movement than to avoid it. I think that our prayer is beginning to reflect more closely the unique way in which we do relate at a personal level to God.

In the following sections I would like to look rather briefly at different kinds of prayer that people often find helpful, and how they lead into prayer at this deeper level, and prepare to understand it. They are, as it were, routes that we might follow in learning to pray, and in so far as they are intended to help us connect with God and grow in friendship and commitment to him, they are ways into prayer at the deeper level that will be considered later on.

Formal prayers

My own first lessons in prayer were learnt at my mother's knee, using the simplest of prayers in a prayer book for children; there I learnt the Lord's Prayer too. And I expect most of us begin in some such way, at whatever age we learn to pray. There is a language of prayer that, like all languages, can really only be learnt by listening to it in use, guided and encouraged by others more fluent than ourselves. The language of prayer too has its vocabulary, idioms and grammar, and we can learn this well by using prayers that have become an established part of the 'literature', the classic prayers we can find in any standard prayer book. We really can learn a lot about prayer from putting on our own lips the words that have been hallowed by the prayer of others; at a practical level of faith they teach us better almost than any academic theology how to express our hopes and fears, our needs and joys to God, and how to connect our lives with the great mystery of God's love for us shown in Jesus Christ.

As these prayers enter our spiritual bloodstream, they nourish our minds and hearts and help us make sense of our lives in communion with the faith they express. In practical terms, they can be used as a route into the deeper, more personal prayer I mentioned in different ways. This is particularly true with the traditional prayers we can find in prayer books or collections of prayers. One way to use them is to nourish the language of our own prayers, like foreign language phrase books! Another way is to read them very slowly, as in a meditation, staying silent after each phrase or idea, thinking about its meaning, applying it to our own lives, and turning our mind to God (with or without words) in adoration or praise. They are an excellent guide to the kinds of ways in which we naturally approach God. Another way connected to this is simply to enjoy them, almost like poems, for their own sake, and in that enjoyment to turn ourselves to God and pray from the heart. Such prayers can serve not only as points of departure; they can also be a fallback, especially in dark times, times of anxiety or sickness: at times when we do not find it easy to pray in our own words there is the immense wealth of Christian prayer to support us expressed in the words of others.

A bit like visiting old churches, finding our way around these traditional prayers prepares us for silent prayer by teaching us the shape and resonance of our interior sacred space. There is always a place for this kind of praying, and its value is closely connected to what can be said about liturgical prayer.

Five fingers and a hand

When I was twelve and preparing for Confirmation, one of the most useful lessons I learnt was to be shown five different ways prayer could go. I still thought of prayer as a wordy activity, but coming to understand these traditional styles or genres of prayer was a great help learning to pray in my own words. The five ways were asking God for things – for others as well as for myself; thanking him; saying sorry to him; and praising him for what God is in himself.

The priest who was preparing us used the five fingers of the hand to teach it. The weakest fingers were for asking for people or things (me, on the last finger, being shorter than my neighbour on the fourth). Thanksgiving was on the middle and longest finger; it was the kind of prayer there should be most of. The index finger was for pointing, not to blame others but to acknowledge my own fault. This was the prayer of confession and contrition. The thumb, which can stand alone from the other fingers, was for God himself, the prayer of adoration and praise. I must say the clarity of this pattern I still find enormously helpful, and so easy to use. Above all, perhaps, it helps teach that the most precious part of prayer is praising God just for being himself. The prayer of adoration teaches us simply to worship God, not necessarily saying anything, but just putting ourselves in his presence and staying there for a while 'letting God be God'.

But there was a sixth way of praying I learnt too: the prayer of offering or dedication. I learnt this more for myself when making my thanksgiving after Holy Communion. When I thought how God had literally put himself in my hands, I realized the only way I could say thank you was to offer him my own life in similarly concrete ways. This goes so naturally with adoration. But it opens up prayer as a response to God at the most personal level, the level of our vocation. It teaches us to see ourselves in relation to God, and to wonder what he wants us to do and to be. If we think of the five fingers representing the various kinds of prayers, we could think of this sixth kind as the palm of the hand open to give and to receive.

Later on, when I entered the monastery, the Novice Master used to say there was a Chinese proverb (there are so many!) that we are all born with our hands closed: the whole art of life consists in learning to open them. In the same way the five fingers of prayer help us open the palms of our hands to give ourselves as an offering to God and to receive the gifts he wants to give.

This kind of praying encourages us to use our own words and thoughts in prayer, and gives a simple but excellent structure to integrate a whole range of styles of prayer. It also helps us move beyond discursive thought in prayer to something simpler and more contemplative. It teaches us to put ourselves in God's presence and to listen to him. This is where the fundamental shift in prayer begins which this book is going to explore; for listening puts prayer on a completely different footing. It acknowledges that God is the one who matters far more than anything we have to say. The problem is that, unsurprisingly, listening is terribly hard, but that is where there are some vital further lessons to be learnt.

Praying with scripture

Listening in prayer is one of the big lessons we have to learn if we are going to let prayer develop. One of the ways we can learn to do it is by building into our times of prayer some place for the Bible. For Christians, the Bible is God's word to us; it is something we can listen to, even if we are reading it to ourselves, and by doing this we more naturally learn to pray to God within a two-way relationship, and gradually in a relationship where God can have the first word. For anyone who wants to take prayer seriously this is a crucial lesson to learn; we will never find God if we insist on doing all the talking.

Bible reading helps us in a number of ways. First, it teaches us the great story of faith into which Jesus was born and in which he was brought up. It shaped his own horizons of faith and hope, and for us who look to Jesus as 'the pioneer and perfecter of our faith' (Heb. 12.2) it is a vital part of our own education in faith to learn to see things with his eyes and his imagination. So not only the New Testament but also the Old Testament have a lot to teach us in various ways.

But reading the Bible wisely is not a straightforward matter. It is worth using some reading guides to help get our bearings. There are many excellent tools here. There are a number of structured reading notes, and commentaries; some encyclopedias have very useful information in them, and particularly to be recommended are editions of the Bible that have introductions, running titles, cross-references and footnotes. All these aids give much needed help in approaching the text in the right kind of way. But each of us must find his or her own way around, and try to develop a personal familiarity and rapport with the Bible. I would nearly always recommend a beginner to start with the Gospels in order to get to know Jesus Christ, and then perhaps move on to the Acts and the New Testament Letters, to glimpse how people first tried to express their faith in Jesus and the kind of Christian church community it shaped.

But, although it requires some perseverance, the aim

over the long haul should be to get stuck into the whole Bible story, to try to understand the characters, and engage with the enormous ups and downs of it all, all the time trying to tune into the way a whole people's understanding of God and his purposes was shaped by the experience of thousands of years. In my last year at school I used to help in a parish in Birmingham where the priest said simply that the Old Testament, read in the light of the New, was one of the best introductions there was to pastoral theology as it helped us understand the ways of God in human history as well as the ways people grow in his knowledge and love.

But beyond this kind of thoughtful Bible reading, we need to feed on it even more personally in prayer. There are various ways in which prayer can be linked to reading and meditation. Three ways have been particularly fruitful. The oldest is the traditional practice of *lectio divina*, which is often associated with monastic spirituality, but which is actually implicit in the liturgical traditions of Christianity and goes back into ancient ways of engaging with a sacred text. Here the idea is simply to try, in the quiet of one's own prayer, to take to heart a passage of the Bible in the simple belief that it is a word of God personally addressed to oneself, almost as if we could hear God or Jesus reading the words to us. As we chew the words over and digest them, not only with our minds but drawing them down into our hearts, we try to tune into the kind of response they evoke in us, the way we hear them addressing us in our own life situation. Out of this response we turn to God in prayer, and either with words or just in a silent movement of the heart, place before him ourselves, our life, our joys, our hopes and fears. And finally we just think about him, and express our love for him in a simple act of contemplative prayer.

Another way of using the Bible is in a rather different kind of meditation exercise, sometimes called Ignatian meditation. In this kind of meditation a person tries to engage imaginatively with a story or an episode in the Bible at a profoundly personal level, trying to find themselves in it, exploring the scene from the inside of the story, as it were, and always examining their reactions, the movements of their hearts. Although this is less formally a conversation in prayer than *lectio divina*, and it encourages a freer kind of psychological exploration of the story rather than a dialogue with the text, in practice this style of meditation is close to *lectio divina* in that the Bible story becomes a kind of safe space to allow a person to open their heart and discern the spirit that is moving in them, and find an environment of prayer in that process.

Finally some people who have begun to respond to the call to a more contemplative way of praying with scripture can find a method known as Centering Prayer useful. In modern times this has been particularly associated with the Cistercian monk, Fr Basil Pennington. Centering Prayer, however, uses a very traditional approach which we find described in the Conferences on Prayer (Conferences 9 and 10) by John Cassian in the late fourth to early fifth centuries. The anonymous mid-fourteenth-century English mystical treatise, *Cloud of Unknowing*, gives very similar advice. In this approach, a phrase or word from a Bible passage (but it could be from anywhere) which has in some sense 'spoken' to someone is used in meditative prayer either as a kind of plumb line to deeper prayer by being gently repeated as and when it is needed to keep the heart awake and focused on God or as an anchor, to keep us rooted in attention to him whom we worship in the silence of our hearts.

Spiritual reading

The Bible has come to play a much more central part in people's education in prayer in recent decades. In an earlier age the important thing was to do 'spiritual reading'. This formed the raw material for meditation, which was understood as a way of pondering prayerfully on the truths of faith, or of one's own life of faith, and of the ways of God. Such meditation was often based on a number of 'points' for reflection and prayer that were drawn out of such reading. This approach has certainly been a sure and tested method of prayer. Its chief strength must be the serious recognition it gives to the place of the mind and understanding in developing good habits of prayer. Nevertheless, prayer tends to move from the mind to the heart, and traditionally it was recognized that, once the heart was more securely set on the things of the Spirit, the time would come to move beyond such structured meditation to something more affective (as it was called), or from the heart.

I am not sure how common this method is nowadays. Perhaps because of higher levels of secular education, the sharpening of a more sceptical and critical style of reason, as well as a more hectic and demanding way of life, people often seem to start the journey of prayer in need of something else. In addition, a generally better understanding of the faith and, I am sure, a more intelligent and personal style of participation in the liturgy, mean that the kind of head-work the older methods of meditation trained is not needed in the same kind of way by many. Meditation in the more contemporary sense of techniques of keeping quiet and tuning in to a deeper level of awareness and imagination is for many a more congenial way to approach prayer.

On the other hand, spiritual reading is still important. We cannot expect to grow in our faith if we do not educate our minds in the things of God, or try to deepen our understanding of the Church and sacraments, which provide and nourish our communion in faith. It is a good thing too to read the lives of saints and other examples of the Christian life, as well as their own writings. To be sure, reading to inform the mind, however necessary, is not itself prayer, but as we come to understand things more clearly or fully, it is certainly going to be easier to let prayer grow and deepen. We will learn to let our ideas of God and of his ways of working enlarge, and we will avoid the risk of prayer dying on us for lack of nourishment. The key is to make sure to let reading turn to prayer, either in a struc-tured but prayerful reflection on points arising in our reading, or just by thinking how what we have been reading connects with God and then turning our hearts and minds to him.

The Rosary

The Rosary is an ancient way of prayer, and is a devo-tion particularly characteristic of the Roman Catholic tradition. Many prayer books explain how to say the Rosary, and here I want to say something about its value as a route into prayer. But to do so, something must be said about the place of Mary, the mother of Jesus, in Christian prayer and devotion.

In the Catholic tradition, Mary can never be separated from her Son. She is the human being closest to him as his mother; she is also the one most closely engaged, by her faith, hope and love, in the mystery of our salvation; the one who meditated constantly on the life and teaching of her Son, the one who shared most deeply in the agony and the ecstasy of his Passion and Resurrection. In the Acts of the Apostles (1.14), she was at the centre of the fledgling Christian community where it is described as being 'constantly devoted to prayer', and she is often depicted at Pentecost sitting at the centre of the apostles when the Holy Spirit was given to the Church. It is this centrality of Mary to the life of faith and the life of prayer that gives the Rosary its special place in Catholic devotion.

Essentially the Rosary is a way of joining Mary in her meditation on the mystery of Christ, as well as sharing her journey along the path of her Son's life, death and Resurrection to the hope and glory of heaven. The tenfold repetition of the Hail Mary could seem to distract attention from Jesus to her. But that is to miss the point. In the first part of the Hail Mary we join the angel Gabriel and her cousin Elizabeth in their double salutation of Mary at the outset of the human life of Jesus in the Annunciation and Visitation. In those episodes she accepted her particular role in the story of our salvation, not only in becoming the Mother of God, but also in her spontaneous concern for others. Both in her turning to God and her turning to us, she brings Jesus to us and is the mother of us all. Our greeting of Mary similarly is an expression of our turning ourselves to the child she bears. In the second part of the Hail Mary, on the other hand, we acknowledge her honour as the Mother of God and quietly ask her to pray for us and with us to him who is our Lord and hers.

As with any method of praying, the Rosary can be used in various ways, and one of its merits is the flexibility with which it adapts itself to different levels of praying. At its simplest it is a form of vocal prayer with meditation on the successive mysteries of the Rosary. But the repetitive element of prayer can become much less significant as our meditation deepens; the words, in the back of our minds, even dropping away to a virtually silent 'telling' of the beads can function just to keep us focused on the main task, the turning of our minds and hearts to our Lord. If we want to widen the range of our meditation, we can use this method of praying with other parts of the life of Jesus, and with all sorts of passages of scripture. Or with none at all: we just turn our minds and hearts to God silently, the words or the beads just in the background, ready to keep stray thoughts at bay.

The Jesus Prayer

The Jesus Prayer is even simpler than the Rosary, and its origins are usually traced to Orthodox traditions of teaching on prayer. Its simplicity is that a single prayer provides the pattern of words, 'Lord Jesus Christ, Son of God, have mercy on me'; many find it easier as the prayer is simply addressed to Jesus himself. Again there is flexibility, in that the basic pattern can be amplified into a kind of litany of the different names of Christ, as for example 'Lord Jesus Christ, born for us . . . , . . . crucified for us . . .' Like the Rosary, it can be used as a kind of background to a specific meditation on the life of Christ. But typically its virtue is the way that it readily falls into the background of our prayer as we pray increasingly from the level of our hearts, below the level of our discursive minds. At this level of prayer we will often be glad of something that can keep our minds occupied in a sympathetic way, but without it really occupying our attention too much, if at all, so that our attention can turn to God and dwell on the thought of him.

In recent times, particularly associated with the name of John Main and his disciple, Laurence Freeman, various other kinds of 'mantra' prayer have been promoted. I think that the same can be said about them as about the Rosary and, perhaps even more so, the Jesus Prayer. In contrast to things that are sometimes said about the importance of persevering with repetition of the formula, I would say that, whatever form the mantra takes, it is only ever a tool or an instrument to help us pray. For people who live in a noisy or disorganized world, it can be a vital anchor, keeping us to the task, and faithful to prayer. But it is never an end in itself, and we should be flexible in our use of it; we should use it as and when it is helpful, but never feel enslaved to it. The function of the tool is to free the heart to pray, and that prayer is something that is given to it from the Spirit; it is not conjured up by our efforts or discipline in following any particular method.

Litanies

Litanies are a less common style of prayer now, perhaps, than in earlier times. But they too can be a very useful way of developing a simple, repetitive kind of prayer which keeps the mind focused but gives the heart a greater measure of freedom to follow its supernatural instinct to turn to God. The successive acclamations form a concise kind of meditation on the theme of the litany, but with almost no discursive content: each point is expressed purely as an acclamation of worship. It is in such an atmosphere that we learn adoration and praise.

Liturgical prayer

So far we have considered various ways in which people can develop good habits of personal prayer on their own. But more and more often, I think, people who have begun to take prayer seriously turn to the liturgical prayer of the Church. This can be by sharing in the Eucharist more frequently during the week; or by sharing in the Prayer of the Church, also called the Liturgy of the Hours, which is the regular pattern of offices, morning and evening, by which people try to consecrate their day to God in communion with the official daily prayer of the Church. Even when they say these on their own or meditate on the daily readings of the Eucharistic liturgy, the fact that they are able to share in the Church's great work of public prayer is a great source of strength and encouragement.

Liturgical prayer is a wonderful school of prayer because it is the prayer of the Church and is rooted in the communion of faith not only now, but also through the ages. It teaches us we are never on our own, always part of something beyond quantifying; we only ever pray as members of the Church, and as parts of the Body of Christ and in the power of the Holy Spirit. The liturgy is the environment in which the life of prayer is most obviously and completely itself. It is where we can learn to pray as Christians, and it should also be the summit of our prayer.

The great virtue of the Liturgy of the Hours, or the Divine Office, is the simple structure it gives for supporting prayer through a whole day, and keeping the working day pointing towards God. It also uses the rhythm of the liturgical year and of the saints' days, which means that daily prayer can be shaped by the great rhythms of the Church's celebration of the mysteries of our faith. Its official character means that people who use it can readily feel that they are not alone in their prayer and it is, of course, very easy to use when people want to pray together – there has been too much emphasis in the past on prayer as a solo exercise – and it goes hand in hand with the day-to-day celebration of the Eucharist.

At a time when people easily feel spiritually adrift in a culture unsympathetic to Christian faith and values these virtues are enormously important. On the other hand, it can happen that after enjoying an initial benefit from this way of prayer, the routine element in it begins to take over; it is still something good to do, but it is hard to appreciate the way it nourishes personal prayer. This is a characteristic problem with any formal pattern of prayer, and the danger is that we try to recover the initial enjoyment by trying to do more and more things when we really need to change our approach, possibly even doing less rather than more, but learning to engage with prayer at a deeper level than hitherto.

To do this the very structure of the Office helps in giving a framework we can adapt to our own needs. Basically it varies little from Hour to Hour, and teaches us to open our hearts to receive the word of God and let the themes of our own prayer be shaped by our response to that word. The initial verses and hymn help us get ourselves back together and place us in God's presence; they also highlight a specific time of prayer and identify its sacred character, be it the time of day, the day of the week, feast or time of the year. It is important for us to make a break with our everyday time and space, and anything we can do to create a hallowed space to pray in will be a help.

The Psalms that follow in the Office, and which form the major element in it, open up a wide range of human emotions and approaches to God. They do not necessarily chime in with the way we feel at any given moment ourselves, but over a period of time they can help us learn to express our whole selves to God rather than just our 'good' selves. They also put us in touch with people of all sorts and conditions, and express our solidarity with them. The Psalms have been called a mirror of the soul: they can help us as well as anything can to accept ourselves, or at least face up to ourselves in prayer; we can certainly be left puzzled and embarrassed by the 'difficult' Psalms, but they all help to inculcate an honesty we need in prayer. Only so can we be open to God.

But the Psalm is not itself the prayer; some of them certainly are, when we make them our own, but their chief function in the Office is to open us up to prayer in response to God's word. Their end point is to prepare us to receive the word of God in the scripture reading, which can be short or long depending on the time of day. This is the true centre of each Hour, and it is a very good habit to learn to rest silently after it, to let it sink in. The Responsory that follows can then express something more personal from our own hearts. At the major Hours (Lauds, Vespers and Compline) this passes into the joy of one of the gospel canticles before turning to petitionary prayer, the Lord's Prayer and Collect. The conclusion too has the function of bringing us out of the sacred time of the Hour of prayer and helping us return to the duties and demands of our ordinary life.

The key to making the Office our own as prayer is to let the 'official' texts breathe together with the breath of our own spirits. That is to say, we should try to make them as personal as possible, and be ready to take time over them. We can take the texts quite meditatively and let them breathe in to us; and we can use them to breathe out ourselves in prayer as well. Only clergy are obliged to say the whole Office; it is not essential to finish a particular office, or to go through everything. It will never be prayer if it becomes a performance, or just something to be got through. So people must not be afraid to let the Spirit guide them in the way they use the Office, above all when they feel inclined to put the book aside and pray silently from time to time.

Moving on

These are only a few ways in which people may find a route into prayer. In various ways they all have a contribution to make towards learning how to pray, and grow in a sense of the possibilities of prayer, especially in teaching us how to pray the Liturgy of the Church. Each of them helps us learn to discover what I called our God-wardness and how we can in some way make that orientation a means of communication between God and ourselves. But I think that in different ways each of them tries to take us beyond words into a deeper kind of communication in prayer, where things can seem much less secure and predictable. For when we are seeking God, we have to learn to tune into a very different kind of eloquence.

Further reading

David Foster (ed.), *Downside Prayerbook* (London, Burns & Oates, 1999)

David Foster, *Reading with God: Lectio Divina* (London, Continuum, 2005)

Gerard Hughes, *God of Surprises* (London, Darton, Longman and Todd, 1996)

André Louf, *Teach us to Pray* (London, Darton, Longman and Todd, 1974)

Basil Pennington, *Centering Prayer: Renewing an Ancient Christian Prayer Form* (New York, Bantam, Doubleday Dell Publishing Group, Reprint edition 1982)

Basil Pennington, *Lectio Divina: Renewing the Ancient Practice of Praying the Scriptures* (New York, Crossroad Publishing, 1998)

Setting out on the journey

2

However we pray, we are, I think, likely to notice some changes over time in the way prayer 'goes'. Often we will need to adjust to a sense that it doesn't! To some extent trying out various methods of prayer can help in different ways to adapt to things. But in general, I believe there is a deeper process of growth taking place that calls for patience. We need to take time to take in the sense of a deepening relationship with God and to learn how to adapt to what is happening. In particular, we can find we are having a problem with the words or whatever we do to pray. It is not that we don't want to pray, or that we are hard put to begin to pray, but when we do we are overcome with a sense of not being able to get down to it, a sense of distaste or boredom with it, or of feeling it is a waste of time. This is the point at which I think this shift in prayer is beginning to take place. The familiar methods lose their impact because the prayer we are actually being drawn to has less and less to do with the words or patterns we have been using. It is shifting to our hearts, and to that extent it is slipping out of our conscious control. Characteristically, we will also find that listening becomes more important than what we may try to say or think we should. Most often words still have a part to play in our praying but, beneath it all, the shift is beginning to take place that I have described as a shift from 'prayers' to prayer.

This distinction is in no way to deny the validity of praying in the way of 'saying prayers'. The distinction is between 'prayers' as something we can do and 'prayer' as something we can't. This shift marks an important discovery: prayer is not something we can make; it is not a procedure. We discover that prayer is essentially God-given, and we need to learn that in an important way it is something God does in us.

At this stage we need to be able to rely on a certain discipline or habit of mind and heart that can be overlooked at the outset. Consequently, this chapter aims to do little more than rehearse some basic practical points about prayer. They will hardly be new to anyone who is used to praying. But I think it is worth putting things as straightforwardly and practically as possible – a kind of revision class – since even people who are used to prayer can need to go back to basics when they find themselves being drawn more deeply into prayer. There are some basic truths about prayer that deserve to be spelled out first, before considering some basic rules or practical principles I think are useful to help prayer flourish at a deeper level.

Three truths about prayer

1 We need to pray

St Isaac of Nineveh in the seventh century commented that birds sing, fish swim, and human beings pray. Prayer is a human being's characteristic activity and we are diminished without it. We need prayer like birds need air and fish water to do what they do and to flourish in being what they are. But there is this difference: in our case, prayer does not seem like that to start with. We often find that prayer goes against the grain. On the other hand, it is only in praying that we learn our need of prayer, and are able to let it open up for us the broader dimensions of spiritual existence in which we can truly flourish. In that, prayer is actually little different from discovering the natural benefits of making an effort about anything, be it physical exercise or mental activity, like reading or listening to music. It is the same spiritually with prayer; without it we remain spiritually stunted and deprived. Unlike our bodily needs, which can all be satisfied, prayer will never satisfy our spiritual need. In prayer we only discover that our need for prayer goes on and on and on. We have to learn to be perpetually dissatisfied. But we can learn that this is what gives our lives that without which we could not otherwise live. For we have learnt to dwell not on ourselves but on God.

This truth demands, then, that we be ready to make prayer a priority in our daily life. It does not mean that we do the impossible, but that we do what we need to live our lives Godwards. We may have to face some challenges here to our overall system of priorities. Prayer cannot be an add-on; and there is no real scope for self-pity or excuses. Whatever reason there may be for letting prayer dwindle and our spirit suffocate, we have to take responsibility for the necessary changes to address this. Prayer in a busy life is possible, because God is always closer to us than we are to ourselves; but we have to learn how to live from the heart, so that prayer can become fully integrated into our lives and so that we know how to tune into something that is always part of our deepest selves.

2 We learn to pray by praying

We do not have to read the right books, find the best guru, or attend courses. These can turn out to be ways of trying to compensate for the frustration we get actually praying; they can even be an evasion. To pray, we just need to start praying. However we set about it, no single way is ultimately better than another. All of them are only routes into something where we are not in charge; it is never a performance. We can only pray . . . and want . . . and try . . . to pray.

Nor are there special techniques of prayer for advanced souls. Prayer is not a matter of that kind of expertise. In this sense, prayer is not just something we do like fish in swimming or birds in singing. It is relational. The characteristically human activity is something we discover in the way we enter into relationships with each other, and supremely in learning to love. Prayer is the way we engage in friendship and love with God and, through him, with the world and with other people. There is something we have to learn here; not a technique, but how to give ourselves more generously to God and to others. As human beings we cannot love from our own resources; we only learn to love in response to love. So prayer is nourished by learning to be loved by God and to accept his mercy and grace. But this means we also need to recognize our tendency to avoid the demands of God's love, our resistance to him, our subterfuges and deceits. As St John learnt, the truth is not that we love God, but that he first loved us (1 Jn 4.19). We need to pray to let that truth become a living part of ourselves.

God is the only real teacher in prayer, and we learn from him by letting him teach us while we pray, by sitting at his feet as Mary, the sister of Martha, did (Lk. 10.38–42). More than that, we have to learn that prayer is God's gift, and the frustrating point where we discover we cannot pray is where we have to learn to let the Holy Spirit do the praying in us. What we have to learn is how to collaborate with the work of the Spirit. Briefly, our task is to keep ourselves patiently at the work of prayer, however it goes or seems not to go, and patiently to dismantle all obstacles that stand in the way. When the disciples asked Jesus to teach them to pray (Lk. 11.1ff.), we perhaps ought to be puzzled that someone who was profoundly a man of prayer had spent so long with his disciples without doing so. But it is as if he had expected them to pick it up just by being with him. Prayer is something that comes through keeping company with Jesus. There can be no better way than that, and ultimately there can be no other!

3 Prayer involves work

Prayer is God's gift to us, something he does in and through us. But we still have to make the effort. It is most characteristically, properly and fully the work of human beings. But it is not like any other work we do. It is not productive work, in which we become more and more efficient and productive. It is a gift. God gives it freely and undeserved to those who seek it. Our work is to receive that gift; we can never deserve it. But like friendship, it is something we have to work at. Prayer is a relationship, and it grows by the attention we pay to it.

A classic problem in prayer is that we habitually carry on relating to God as babies or youngsters even when we are old. We don't grow up spiritually. Grown-up relationships make demands, and only by meeting the demands others make on us, by our commitment to them, do relationships mature and bear fruit. So we can only get good at prayer by getting more and more deeply involved with God, and by letting him help us grow up into the person he wants us to be. We are created in the image and likeness of God. In some way each of us reflects something of God himself. Prayer is a vital part of letting that become the way we look. It is a way of letting God tell us who we are.

There is a side to prayer that can seem hard work. But it is when we are ready to work hard at it that we can also discover its spontaneity, when prayer comes easily, joyfully and naturally. The two kinds of prayer do not necessarily come at the same time. But there is a connection between them deep down. It is the time we are ready to devote regularly to prayer each day, and the sacrifices we are ready to make for it, that prepare our heart to respond more easily in prayer to the initiatives God takes towards us in the rest of the day. It is easy to be too prescriptive here. But on the whole I think it is wiser to look for time for regular prayer in the morning than in the evening. That is when our minds and hearts are less cluttered and, even if we don't really feel our best, it is easier to devote ourselves more completely to God. It does not need to be a long time, but a time we can be faithful to; something that can be a reference point for the rest of the day. It is not how we feel that matters, but what we want. The little sacrifices we make to find the space and the time will not pass un-rewarded.

The more prayer becomes a habit of heart and mind, the more spontaneous it gets; it becomes a sort of attitude, a way we have learnt of looking at everything, which guides the way we live and respond to everything. Our work then is to let the work of prayer carry on; to keep the heart open and attentive to God's work in us.

Three basic rules in prayer

When we do pray, and however we set about it, there are a few very simple things I think are always worth bearing in mind. They are rules to which I find myself coming back again and again.

1 Let God be God

This follows on from the fact that prayer is really God praying in us. It is no use making do with anything less than God. We may know a lot about God in terms of theology or the Bible, but to let God be just God in our prayer is altogether more disorientating. He is not anything else or, in fact, any thing at all. In real terms we can have no idea of who or what he is like, although we have all got our own ways of thinking inadequately about him.

Some of our problems with God seem to be really problems with our idea of God. We like to think of him as a kind of Santa Claus, perhaps, or a fairy godmother; or we might think of him as a heavenly policeman, schoolmaster or judge; sometimes we might think we have grown out of that kind of stuff, but try to turn God into a kind of 'buddy', someone whom we imagine we can cuddle up with. The list can go on and on. They are all ways of trying to have God on our own terms, whether to make us feel good or bad, or just safe. We must let go of the ideas we impose on God, whether unconsciously or (with the best will in the world) consciously. The hardest ones are the unconscious ones: we have to be ready to let go of a lot of personal baggage to find ourselves in any kind of real relationship with him. Over the long haul, God shows what is needed. We don't need to get neurotic about it; we just need to be ready to let go of what is not God. We have got to let God be God if we are ever going to survive praying – and to let God be God for us.

2 Let God be God for us

This principle follows from the last. Only in prayer can we give God the time he needs to introduce himself to us.

Prayer is giving God whatever time it takes for him to love us; or rather, for us to accept his love of us and to learn to make that love the mainspring of our lives. Another serious problem in prayer is that we do not let him love us; this is often because we do not know how to love ourselves. If we cannot love ourselves, we will not be able to let others love us, and whatever we feel we have to hide is going to become an obstacle to letting God love us. A major task in prayer is learning self-acceptance, and patience and gentleness with ourselves. This is something we can learn from God, though, in prayer. One way is simply to sit in front of a crucifix, where Jesus is at his most vulnerable and his compassionate love most visible, and learn that God never condemns those who turn towards him, and that whatever we do to him becomes, beyond our imagining, an additional motive for his mercy.

3 Let God take his time

A thousand years are but a twinkle in his eye (2 Pet. 3.8)! Patience is what prayer is all about: patience with others, with ourselves, and with God. Our mistake here is linked to the idea that we have got to be getting things done. Prayer is an activity, but it's not about productivity, reaching goals, or performance: it can only be measured in terms of love. Julian of Norwich (c. 1342–1423) gives wise advice here. She speaks of God's patience with us and his courtesy. It is not that God takes his time so much as that we need time to learn God's ways with us. But we do not need to worry: he sees no ill and all shall be well.

Rooted and grounded in prayer

For all that has just been said, there are some practical things that can help us if we want to encourage the deepening of prayer. They are not a recipe that will guarantee a result; but they are ways to avoid some elementary problems that make prayer difficult, especially for us who live in too busy a world with too much emphasis on doing and producing. The key idea could be summed up in phrases like 'getting focused' or 'finding our centre'. I generally think of them as ways of getting our feet on the ground, the holy ground of prayer, or, in the electrical metaphor, of earthing ourselves. Much of it resembles advice for relaxation, meditation (in the secular sense of a mental discipline) and the like. In these cases, though, our efforts are directed only towards ourselves. For prayer, we are directing our attention and energy towards God. But these techniques can help free up energy and our powers of attention so that we can use them to make the spiritual journey, as it is often called, from the mind to the heart. That goes beyond the *psyche* into the dimension of the spirit. We must not get so absorbed by the techniques and their psychological benefits that we fail to make the inner journey of prayer!

Praying is making that journey; it is the path we follow to reach our centre. Prayer doesn't only start when we have attained this inner freedom, or however it is to be described. Prayer is a matter of desire, and desire is always for something that remains unsatisfied. As the ancients saw it, the heart is the place of prayer, the place where we find God and are able to move beyond ourselves into his love. Even to start the journey is to respond to the pull of his love, and prayer is our response to the pull that makes our hearts restless. There is a restlessness, too, that comes from the way a lot of our prayer involves a struggle with a spiritual culture that is resistant to God, as well as our own frailty and vulnerability, that leave us prey to the pull of sin. The journey of prayer can seem a rather precarious path, when we are very conscious of the 'wobble' in our human nature, which is how Original Sin has been described. We must not worry about this too much; it is just part of being human. As such it is bound to be part of our prayer; and it has the positive function of reminding us to be patient, humble, to let God do the work we cannot do. As St Peter realized when he started to drown, he only had to look at Jesus to be able to walk on the water (Mt. 14.22-33).

The key idea behind getting our feet onto the ground of prayer is to learn how to change the focus of our attention to a level of spiritual awareness deeper than the ordinary level of everyday sense perception and practical thinking. It is at a level deeper, too, than our emotions, a level where we can get in touch with our whole being, and more deeply in touch, too, with our inner and outer worlds. This is the deeper spiritual reality we call our heart – the centre of our being where God dwells. To learn how to tune into things at this level is how we can foster and cultivate a sense of the presence of God and make his presence felt for others.

Although notions like being grounded, centred or focused are only metaphors for a method of getting into prayer, they say a lot about what we are trying to do at a deeper level. It is an idea used a lot by Thomas Merton, and others who have been influenced by him, and it means much more than just a kind of prayer. It includes human integrity and the spiritual maturity that shows in our openness to things and our availability to people, our ability 'to be there for them'. Someone who is grounded is stable, a source of stability for others. As with the notion of an electrical earth, such a person can prevent short-circuiting. A centred kind of person is someone who has achieved the kind of self-knowledge that only grows out of being connected in a spiritual dimension with the source of our being, however that is understood. In this context, being focused also speaks of a degree of clarity of our awareness with which we can see others and ourselves in a less ego-centred way. But the fundamental attitudes of attention, trust and reverence that are involved here are ones that we learn best of all in prayer.

Getting into the here and now

Putting it as simply as possible, this grounding process means three things: getting into the here and now; getting our minds back into our bodies; and learning to stay there! This is important because, as far as we are concerned, God is exclusively in the here and now; he is always with us, but we habitually fail to notice the signs of his presence. So in order for prayer to be a genuine communication with him, we need to cultivate in our lives of prayer what Jean-Pierre de Caussade called the 'sacrament of the present moment'. And this calls for certain habits of body and mind.

As far as the body is concerned we can learn a lot from yoga or, less exotically, from the basic relaxation exercises we can pick up in leaflets at the doctor's surgery. The point in our case, however, is not to relax for its own sake, but to minimize the interference the body can cause to our attention when we are trying to deepen it and focus it on God, that most elusive aspect of our experience. Someone called this learning the art of sitting still; that is to say, sitting in a relaxed but alert way, the way world-class soloists compose themselves before a performance. Even without a performance to carry off, such bodily composure helps to attune the mind and heart, so that, in whatever way we are called on, we are able to respond attentively and gently; to be able to pick up subtleties in our conversation partner's words and manner; perhaps to be able to discern, even, what is not being said.

Posture is an important element here. Sitting down is perhaps easiest. If we are sitting down we need to sit in the back of the seat, so that our back is well supported, but not so upright as to prevent the spine taking its naturally curved position. Both feet must be on the ground, the legs apart so that the knees are about the same distance apart as our shoulders, and as best we can with the knee joint at a right angle. The upper body should be well balanced; the two shoulders hanging from the collar of the neck as freely as possible, so that the hands can rest in the lap or, as some prefer, on the thighs. In either case it is best for the palms of the hands to face up, for the fingers to be as relaxed as possible. This should allow the neck to assume a relaxed position, at its full extent without being stretched unnaturally. Ideally, people describe the head as feeling like a ball being held on the top of a fountain of water! Whether the eyes are closed or not seems in fact to be unimportant so long as their gaze is not distracted. It helps to learn to let the gaze rest slightly above the midpoint of the line of vision. If the eyes are closed, theoretically the gaze would be above the line where the eyelids are gently joined.

Writing out such a description makes it seem unnecessarily complicated; and, to repeat, this is only a technique to retrieve a healthy sense of bodily presence, which we habitually lose in our drive to run our lives as well as other people's lives for the sake of our own agenda. This drive (or is it drivenness?) is inimical to real prayer. To a great extent the value of such an exercise is preliminary to prayer and certainly could be left aside after settling down in order just to pray. I expect that once the underlying ideas have become second nature, and we know from within how to get back into ourselves, we will be wisest not to be too fastidious about it. However, I do think it is a help for beginners.

Some people prefer kneeling, or standing, or lying on the ground, prostrate or on their backs. Each of these postures can express a personal disposition for prayer and have its own eloquence. In each case the same ideas can be adapted. I would advise people to learn to be still before they explore the analogous possibilities of slow motion. But the Bible suggests ways in which walking, running and leaping for joy also express a prayerful heart!

As we learn to sit still, we could well take some time to pay attention to our physical senses. If we can pay attention to being in a particular place, we are not there as inert lumps, but as sentient beings. What we see, what we hear, the sense of feeling (at least in our backsides!) are part of us; and so is the taste in our mouths, the smell of the air. It can all be something to enjoy, something we may not have realized was there to be enjoyed; or it may be not so good. But it is by being aware of it, and trying to be as gentle as possible in accepting our awareness of it, that we will learn to integrate it into our time of prayer. Or it will just become a distraction we will have to accept later on in our prayer.

So often we ignore our bodies, or rather we just take them for granted, paying them the minimum of attention in terms of personal hygiene. Or we go to the opposite extreme and show an obsession with our physical appearance, fitness and so on. This is as unhealthy for a spiritual life as paying them no attention. It is not a real concern for the body but rather it disguises a preoccupation with how we look and a need to impress others, or ourselves. This is narcissism, and it is also inimical to prayer. But a real awareness of ourselves is rooted in our physical presence and includes our sense awareness. Acknowledging it, and making it part of ourselves, is part of getting into the here and now where we find God.

Getting our minds back into our bodies

Together with getting the body into the here and now, we need to work with our minds. Ultimately prayer involves drawing our minds into our hearts. But before we can do that we need to gather our minds back together into ourselves. This may be harder than we think; for we are compulsively hyperactive, and mentally and emotionally all over the place as a result. We cannot pay proper attention to things, even immediate things. It is much worse when it comes to God.

A symptom of our problem can be found, for example, in the brevity of film sequences used to build up the narrative line of television soap operas. This is an indication of the extremely short attention spans we now have. In contrast we could think of the difficulty we have sustaining our attention over the chapters and subplots of the classic novels that provided the popular entertainment before television. Spiritually, then, we face a major task when we try to slow down and get our minds fully into the here and now. In our imaginations we inhabit an extraordinary range of places (both real and fantasy places), worrying about so many things, dreaming about countless others, be it in daydreams or nightmares.

So slowing down is essential to our spiritual health. If we can learn how to do so, we will be able to listen better and to notice things that otherwise we never stay around long enough to see. Nature programmes on television, for example, often use slow motion photography to help us concentrate on the details of a process that we never get a chance to appreciate. Learning how to pay that kind of attention, and in a similar way to see what is going on as a whole, is part of what we need to learn by getting into the here and now.

Two aphorisms may help us keep what we have to try to do in mind. As aphorisms, they are well worn but none the less true for that:

Let bygones be bygones;
Let tomorrow look after itself.

We can use them almost as mantras as we begin to sit still and take in the 'here and now'. As we let the flotsam and jetsam drift off and other things settle to the bottom of the water we can begin to get beneath the surface and look into the depths.

But typically we find our minds drifting off with the junk. Stuff from the past, preoccupations with the future, even distractions about the present will all have a go at carrying our attention away. All we can do is to draw our minds, as simply and patiently as possible, back to the here and now. Let bygones be bygones; let tomorrow look after itself. We need, consciously and gently, to come back to ourselves, and every time we start to run after our thoughts again, gently and patiently to bring ourselves back again. It can be difficult to start with, but practice helps a lot. It is not so much a question of learning to concentrate hard on anything; the problem really is that there is nothing to concentrate on, which is why anything else will have a field day. Gentleness and good humour is always needed – it is an education in humility; getting cross with oneself is always counter-productive.

Learning to stay still

Once we have begun to come back to ourselves, both in our minds and bodies, we are in a much better position to turn our attention to God in prayer. Bluntly, to do this we need to stop thinking, and simply turn ourselves towards God instead and learn to want him, nothing else and nothing less than him. The danger here is of taking too forceful or even aggressive an approach to this; it is better just to let our thinking come to a stop. The key insight of the fourteenth-century English mystical treatise, the *Cloud of Unknowing,* which will be looked at more closely in the next chapter, is that we reach God by loving him not by our thinking. The mind can feed our love. But prayer is about loving God, which means we need to let ourselves move away from the thought of God to God himself. Or rather we can try to let the thought of God move us to love.

But this is to anticipate the subject of the next chapter. For the time being, something needs to be said about how to stay still. For however still we can be, it is always precarious! It is God's way of reminding us to learn to look to him and continually to let him be the source of our prayer. Nevertheless, if we are attentive and loving, we can learn to live with the wobble, which shows itself in various ways.

The most striking problem is one some people have when they pray, of falling asleep! It must at once be said that this may be because a person needs more sleep. It is important to be honest and realistic about this. Conversely, it may be that they need more fresh air and exercise. In other words, there is a danger of people ignoring their mental and physical needs, so that the body kicks in with its demands for rest as soon as they begin to slacken their grip on their conscious lives.

One reason for the difficulty is that when we try to enter into ourselves to pray, the process is very similar to when we fall asleep. We are much more familiar with sleeping than with praying, and sleep is an instinctive response. But we need to learn the other response too. This calls for some discipline to redress the balance, especially if we are trying to pray at unsocial hours – which often happen to be the best suited for it. In other words, as we enter into ourselves to pray, we need to learn to spot the point on the road where, as it were, there is a fork in the road between one road leading to sleep and the other road leading to awareness. It is easy to miss the right turning, and repeatedly, sometimes, we have to come back a little to the signpost and make sure we turn away from oblivion. Again a practical tip is to keep the word 'awake' or 'aware' in our minds to keep us on the right track.

A much more everyday wobble is that caused by so-called distractions. They arise from our thoughts, memories, anxieties, or from other feelings. The name 'distractions' rather over-glamorizes the problem, and I think they are better just called 'interferences' or 'disturbances'. This does not solve the problem, but it does keep it in proportion. It is simply a fact that our minds are easily disturbed; things get in the way, like the crackle and other radio broadcasts we pick up on a radio receiver when we try to tune into a distant station. We are transient and volatile creatures, and this is just part of the way our minds work. The problem is not that things turn up in our consciousness, but that we think about them. The problem is not that we notice them, but that we let them pull us away from simple awareness. Herbert McCabe referred to them as our real wants breaking in. This is a helpful insight, to a great extent because it reminds us to be honest and to 'own' our distractions rather than see them as alien intrusions into 'my' prayer. We need to use the experience as a humbling one and learn to remember our underlying want of God and to try to prefer that.

We need to keep on coming back to ourselves, and keep on patiently turning ourselves towards God. If that feels similar to standing precariously on one foot like the statue of Eros in the middle of London's Piccadilly Circus, so be it. Mindfulness of God means forgetfulness of all that is not God. And this is a process not a state. Prayer is a process of continually minding God in the midst of everything else. Minding him, seeking him, wanting him, preferring him.

There is another kind of problem, rather the opposite of distractions, which is a kind of spiritual wool-gathering, where we content ourselves with thinking of nothing in particular. This seems to me to be a kind of inadvertence to God that leaves our minds ready to think of anything without any discrimination. The problem can arise naturally. For while we need to keep our minds and hearts focused on God, God is, as John Chapman neatly put it, nothing in particular. But for all that, prayer is about continually minding God and training our minds and hearts on him. It is not daydreaming. To me, this difficulty betrays a person's loss of desire. It is a kind of quiet despair or complacency, which calls for some renewal of our minds. It denotes a loss of energy and focus such as arises at a physical level from poor diet or malnourishment. Here it might indicate a loss of appetite whose causes are more profound.

At a low level the difficulty will almost be one of boredom, and can be addressed as such. Generally the problem of the boredom says more about the person complaining of it; the remedy is learning to take the right kind of interest. And an essential step here is not to blame God, but to accept the way we feel and patiently try to take an interest in God, even though he eludes our intelligent understanding. Higher up the scale of seriousness is the problem traditionally called 'aridity', and we have to get used to living without any felt reward for the effort we put into prayer. We have to learn at some stage that God is God, and is not going to be reduced to any interest we have or may take in things. He is uncompromisingly himself. But we have to remind ourselves that what feels like emptiness or absence here is actually the very opposite, that God is with us, and giving himself to us, albeit in ways we cannot feel, understand or appreciate. At its extreme, this experience poses a metaphysical and theological challenge, in the face of which we must try not to lose hope; for it is where we learn to live and to pray purely by faith.

Difficulties like these teach us that we need support structures to keep us focused and grounded in prayer. Attention to our physical environment is important, especially if we do not have the luxury of a church or sacred space in which to pray. Visual focuses like icons or other images can help. A burning candle is another possibility, and perhaps a fragrant one can help recruit our sense of smell to the task of keeping us in the here and now. Personally, I find incense too exotic and irritating on the nose, and, on the whole, my senses generally need calming down. For the same reason, I don't think music is very helpful. Noise can be the worst disturbance of all, whereas music can be a source of great peace. But I find it too demanding on my attention to promote the kind of inwardness for prayer I have been describing.

The best way of dealing with noise, and most disturbances, is to learn the knack of noticing them but not paying them any more attention than that. It is rather like noticing a car over there but paying attention instead to me noticing it here and now. Eventually we can learn to pay attention not to the disturbance but to the space and silence in which it occurs, and to prefer that. This is easiest to apply to the exterior disturbances we have been talking about, but I think the knack can be extended to address interior disturbances as well.

Besides these approaches to keeping still, there are others, all of which involve using a powerful word to assist us. This gives our minds something relatively uninteresting with which to work while we are focusing deeper in our hearts in prayer. A mantra, even a practical token word such as those mentioned above, may help. This is where some forms of prayer such as those mentioned in the last chapter, like the Rosary or Jesus Prayer, come into their own. Here words give grist to the mill, which we can leave to clatter on – the image is St Teresa of Avila's (1515–1582) – while the heart wakens to prayer. The general principle, though, to paraphrase St Theophan the Recluse, the Russian mystic (1815–1894), can be stated thus: bind the mind (and its thoughts) with one thought, or the thought of the one only, who is God.

Or, more humorously, there is the story Donald Nichol gives in his book, *Holiness,* of the monkey catcher. If you want to catch the monkeys that are jumping and scream-ing in the tree, it is no use trying to climb the tree with a bag and chase them one by one. The only way is to get a big bunch of bananas, put it at the bottom of the tree and when they come to eat the fruit you can catch them easily, and without making yourself look ridiculous either.

Further reading

Abhishiktananda, *Prayer* (Norwich, Canterbury Press, 2006)

Michael Casey, *Towards God: The Western Tradition of Contemplation* (London, HarperCollins, 1991)

Anthony De Mello, *Sadhana: A Way to God. Christian Exercises in Eastern Form* (New York, Bantam Doubleday Dell; Reprint edition 1984)

Herbert McCabe, 'Prayer', in *God Matters* (London, Geoffrey Chapman, 1987), Chapter 18, pp. 215–25

Thomas Merton, *Contemplative Prayer* (London, Darton, Longman and Todd, 1973)

Approaching the centre   3

A big milestone in prayer is reached when we discover a need to listen rather than to talk in prayer. The main part of the last chapter was intended to help us develop our listening skills, and in this chapter I want to consider what they help promote in our approach to prayer. Above all they cultivate an inner environment where we can find ourselves praying in a different kind of way, in what is habitually called contemplative prayer.

Listening

A crucial stage in the process of learning to pray is to begin to listen. The essential condition for contemplative prayer is the ability to listen, and an appreciation of silence. This story, often attributed to the Curé d'Ars, is well known:

> An old man would sit still in church for hours on end. One day a priest asked him if God ever said anything to him in his prayer.
>
> 'God does not talk. He just listens.'
>
> 'Well, then, what do you spend all this time talking about?'
>
> 'I don't talk either. I just listen.'

Listening is one of the greatest gifts we can share with each other. Think how bad you feel when you are not being listened to, or when you feel you don't have a voice to say what you want to say. What's more, to be listened to means much more than people hearing your words. It involves everything behind the words; better, it involves 'you', the *person* behind the words, including feelings that so often get in the way of what you would really be able to say if you knew how you felt. Listening is difficult because it means paying attention to all sorts of things, which go unexpressed by another person, at a conscious level, cultivating an awareness of what they may scarcely be aware of themselves. Listening is about personal recognition, a sensitivity and appreciation of another in their otherness, giving them the space and time they need to be themselves. A good listener helps someone understand themselves.

We often find listening does not mean listening to words but to what is not being said and how well we listen is certainly not measured by the brilliance of anything we say in reply.

Listening to God is rather odd. He never seems to say anything, and, to be honest, we don't really expect him to! There is a question here, a doubt even, about prayer. How can prayer really be understood as talking to God? Origen, the great Christian teacher of the second century, was very sniffy about people who thought of prayer in this kind of way; for him it was a habit of thinking we should certainly grow out of because it was unworthy of God, who is certainly a much better kind of being than someone with ears and mouth, however spiritual they might be!

With all due respect, I am not so sure about the force of this criticism. God is completely different from human beings and our relationship to our creator is utterly unique, unlike our relationship with other human beings; but had

Origen never thought how remarkable it was even for human beings to communicate with each other? We can see them and see that they've got ears and mouths like us: they talk back when we speak to them and they make sense. But speaking is not just mouthing audibly, and hearing is not just being on the receiving end of noises. In fact the physics involved in a conversation is incidental to communication; communication involves more, even, than language; it calls on our deepest capacities for human understanding, feeling and sympathy – it is about mind, heart and soul. These are aspects of our human nature, but of our interior nature, our spiritual nature: as such, they are not alien to God who is himself the supreme spirit and who created us in his image.

It is, of course, much easier to understand how human beings communicate with and listen to each other than how we communicate with God. We know how we inhabit a world in which language helps us share our thoughts and our own selves with each other. What we find hard is to understand God's unique relationship to us as our creator, in whom we live and move and have our being, just because there is nothing like it. But the world we inhabit is one where we are aware of others as more than what we are physically in contact with, and we understand all kinds of meaning at a personal level beyond the words and sign we use to express them, consciously and unconsciously; in the same sort of way ours is a world in which God is aware and listens, and in which we can talk and listen to him, not because of any ears, eyes or mouth, but because he is our creator and we are in his image. As such, we have to learn to find him as the source of our being in our very hearts.

To listen to God in the relevant sense of the word means a new kind of listening; we have to tune into our hearts, at the centre of our being. This can seem rather strange to begin with, but it does not mean he does not listen. Nor does the fact that God does not talk back mean that he does not answer prayer. God speaks by silence, and he normally answers us, not by addressing us, but by changing us, or by letting us change. One way of putting this is to say he moves our hearts, and leads us to understand something as a response to our prayer. Sometimes our perspective on something begins to change, so that we learn to see things from God's point of view, as it were. Certainly prayer helps us learn to want what he wants and can give us the courage to do something about it. It is important that one of the ways in which God helps us grow up is by not waving magic wands, or running to help like a nanny: he works through our freedom and sense of responsibility; and he does so by illuminating our consciences and awareness, not by saying anything. This is where we discover the creativity of prayer – where God is at work in our hearts, more deeply than in our consciousness. Nothing could be more powerful than this silent word.

So, however odd it may seem, there is a way of making sense of the idea of listening to God in prayer. As with all natural abilities, some seem to be better at listening than others, but we all improve by working at it. This is not always as easy as we might think. To listen to someone means setting aside not only time but also our personal agenda that takes up so much of our mental and emotional space even when we are sitting with someone giving them time. And then we are so quick to judge what we hear rather than listen to the person talking; and what they say triggers off so many trains of our own thought that we end up running around our mental space, not making the other person comfortable in it; even if we can stop ourselves interrupting, there we are practising our own private monologues in our heads.

When we listen to another we can also find ourselves hearing things we often do not want to hear, and then we have our own internal, more or less incoherent discourse to deal with as well! To listen to another person's feelings we have to accept and find some reconciliation with the mess and disorder in our own feelings: our hurts, prejudices, fears and resentments, as well as our attractions, desires and hopes. We have to come to terms with things we would rather avoid – we have to listen to ourselves.

Prayer is the same as any other listening: we can only free up the space needed to give to God by listening to all this other stuff, letting it come to the surface of our consciousness and finding there the personal space which we can give to God. It is a mistake to think prayer is about getting away from all the inner mess, a mistake to think that we have to go somewhere else to find him. That would only mean getting away from ourselves to find him. That's quite impossible. It's all we've got. Self-awareness, however petty or ignoble we find ourselves to be, is the only awareness we have in order to be aware of God.

We must try not to be discouraged by all this. On the contrary I think something rather beautiful is beginning to take place: the silence we find ourselves listening to becomes a space in which we can be ourselves. It is God's gift to us so that we can be there for him. In silence, God is taking the lead in our prayer. It is his way of teaching us who we are, his way of purifying our hearts, his way of giving us time to find reconciliation and healing, to recover integrity and wholeheartedness, the time we need to grow to our full stature in Christ.

Interior and exterior silence

We need silence in order to learn to listen. In the end the silence we need is silence in our hearts. Interior silence takes time to learn. So to start with at any rate, physical, or exterior, silence is a precious condition for prayer. Once we have found the place of silence in our hearts we can pray in all sorts of situations; but that is not where we start, and physical silence is something we always need to return to. Finding a quiet place may be hard, especially in a household with children. But absolute silence is not necessary; it is sufficient to find somewhere quiet enough to be able to listen to more than what is going on all around us. Some people can get a bit neurotic about noise; but the real challenge in prayer is not the noise around us but the noise within. That is what has to be faced next.

As soon as we try to be quiet and listen in prayer we find all sorts of other noises getting on our nerves. Worse than the lawnmowers and mobile phones are the inner disturbances that start clamouring for attention. Learning to be grounded in prayer or spiritually focused means dealing with more than just the kind of disturbances we mentioned in the last chapter. There is a more fundamental level of difficulty, interior disturbances that affect our very capacity to hear and listen – we find we get in the way of ourselves.

This is mental noise. It needs to quieten down to let us make the journey to the heart. We find it in the way we keep running things over in our minds that just interfere with what we are really about when we are trying to pray. The challenge here is really no more than the need to recollect ourselves from the past and the future that has already been mentioned, but the way we keep mulling things over, especially our anxieties and our resentments, as well as our self-admiration and self-pity, is very subtle. It works at deep levels of our conscious and unconscious minds too, and continually surprises us. A lot of this noise stems from our emotional self. It may be the first time we have been able to give any space or time to listen to such feelings, and this side of ourselves often needs a measure of attention for us to be able to accept it as part of us. We have to learn to make it part of our self-offering of prayer.

To learn to be silent, basically we need to move from being aware of whatever may be cropping up in the field of our attention (and it may be anything) to just being aware. Then it does not matter what crops up in our field of attention; we can switch our attention and focus only on the underlying awareness. The fact that the English verb 'to be aware of' expects an object to make normal sense is an indication of the oddity of what we are learning to do. We will notice all sorts of things when we keep quiet, but in prayer we need to learn just to let them be. And whatever I find myself aware of at any moment, I should try to refocus on just being aware. If whatever it is comes from within, an interior disturbance, I need to be very gentle and acknowledge it as part of me, and try to integrate it into the other part of me that is trying to pray. But the thing is always to listen to the silence, to watch the space, beyond. Remember that I want God more, and he loves me for who I am, not for what I am.

Silence itself has many voices! We need to be prepared for the way even our silence discloses unresolved sides of our character. There is the armed silence of anger or hatred, the guarded silence of suspicion. Nervousness encourages yet another kind, the silence of hesitation. For most of us, silence will initially expose much from which we need to be set free in order to pay attention to someone we want to love. It will be God's way of exposing what we often try to conceal by talking and being busy. He will bring all our nervousness and anxiety to the surface; he wants to heal it. This is part of the 'grounding' which is so important a part of praying. As we learn to listen, we may feel there is not much to hear apart from all that stuff getting in the way; but there is something else too. The fact that we are praying means that our desire for God is deeper and more fundamental to our being than anything else. We want God more than however much we want, need (or so we think) or just fancy anything else. We can even learn to prefer the darkness in all this simply because we can be sure that nothing else but the real God will satisfy us – we are not in it for the bright ideas or the feel-good factor.

This is all part of the way we are being made ready for something greater than anything our world, for all its glory, can suggest. Prayer is part of the way God has of teaching us to wait. As we will see later, this kind of prayer involves a purification of our hearts and minds needed for what God promises to those who wait in faith and hope. It lets us deepen our readiness and longing. It can be just a romantic cliché to say that silence means freedom from the bondage of words. But once we have stopped being romantic about prayer, and have learnt to be patient, silence can be a liberating experience in the sense of setting us free for God. It can set us free from the constraints of thought and desire, and from the compulsion to go on talking and thinking, and conjuring up feeling, all of which fall short of God himself. In the end, silence is the atmosphere in which the whole person can be at peace and worship Christ.

We start off our friendship with God by learning the language of prayer, but we can be sure that we will only grow in it by listening to God. Once we recognize that listening is more precious than talking, we need to accept a call to silence in prayer. Prayer comes to mean giving the wordy labour of our minds a rest so that we have a chance to attend to God without worrying about what to say, and without trying to hide behind our speeches and excuses. Silence does not just help us listen. It is characteristic of God's way of communicating with us. Prayer can seem torrid and empty, but the ground of our heart is being made ready for new life. It is a time of growth and of inner transformation. But we need to appreciate that the silence needed for that kind of prayer will get deeper and deeper, and the disturbances will be found less and less in what is outside us, but in what lies in the depths of our heart, and in our very will to pray.

Wisdom from the English mystics

It is perhaps especially when our prayer has reached this stage that we most of all profit from reading other authors on the life of prayer. Among the most helpful are probably the English mystical writers of the fourteenth and fifteenth centuries. They have been mentioned already, but they include the anonymous *Cloud of Unknowing* (mid-fourteenth century), Walter Hilton (*c.* 1343–1396) and Julian of Norwich (*c.* 1342–1423). The *Cloud of Unknowing* has a particularly helpful discussion of the problems we have just been thinking about.

The central image of the *Cloud of Unknowing* refers to the sense of loss of direction, of understanding, of knowing what to do that recurs in our search for God in prayer. But in the Old Testament the Cloud also refers to God's glory and his continuing presence with his people. This is an important insight of the *Cloud of Unknowing*: the Cloud may feel like the absence of God, but it is really his presence, embracing us. The practical corollary is that even if we are only aware of a sense of absence, distance, reluctance or resistance to him, we must simply go on wanting him, simply trusting in his presence. The Cloud is called a Cloud of 'Unknowing' because we often have a lot of 'unlearning' to do, and partly because God is exactly unknowable. Our ideas and expectations of God are going to be continually frustrated and have to be surrendered. In fact our thinking can just become a way of avoiding God, a kind of distraction, and in this case, as with other displacement activities, a welcome one. Instead, we have to give up trying to find out things about God for ourselves, enter the Cloud and just let God take his time with us:

> For though we through the grace of God can know fully about all other matters, and think about them – yes, even the very works of God himself – yet of God himself can no man think. Therefore I will leave on one side everything I can think, and choose for my love that thing which I cannot think! Why? Because by loving he can be caught and held, but by thinking never. (Chapter 6)

The anti-intellectual cast of this advice needs to be taken in context, and it is worth noting the more balanced observation we find in the Augustinian Canon Hilton, whose comments are wholly dependent on St Augustine, that thinking can give us a motive for loving. But even he notes that we can love more than we can know by our rational understanding. And prayer can mean a continual renewal of the act of the will to love God.

Another area where the *Cloud of Unknowing* makes two good suggestions is in discussing distractions of all sorts. Sometimes, the author says we can push them gently aside;

we can use the Cloud as a Cloud of Forgetting and press them down underneath. The focus of our attention should always be what we cannot discern, in the Cloud. Or, when we feel distractions are really pressing in, we can try to look over their shoulders towards God (who is, of course, concealed in the Cloud). It is simple advice, but all the more useful for that.

Julian of Norwich discusses prayer in her Fourteenth Revelation (*Revelations of Divine Love,* Long Text, cc. 41ff.). She is more theological in her approach, and describes the Trinitarian context in which Christian prayer operates through a person's attachment to Jesus Christ. So while she is perfectly clear about the way prayer is centred on Jesus, and on his being the immediate focus of our prayer, God is himself the 'ground of our beseeching'. This should give us confidence and hope, but also a sense of the mysteriousness of what is going on. Prayer is not something in the last analysis that comes from us; there is beneath all that we do a deeper level of causality that finds its origin in God. God moves his creatures to pray because he desires them.

Augustine Baker

One of the people to whom we owe the survival of the *Cloud of Unknowing* is the seventeenth-century English Benedictine monk (by birth, in fact, Welsh), Augustine Baker (1575–1641). Although his writings are finally now being published in modern editions, his best-known book is the compilation of his teaching by Serenus Cressy known as *Holy Wisdom* or *Sancta Sophia* (1657). He makes crystal-clear in this work that we have a single goal in this life which is the perfection that consists in union with God; the value of everything else is relative to that. For our part we must keep this goal continually in sight and strive after nothing less. He picks up and paraphrases the parable of the pilgrim from Walter Hilton, the moral of which is never to give up. The pilgrim has a kind of mantra of his own. He used it in facing down all the difficulties as well as the alluring consolations of the spiritual path, and it is very helpful for anyone:

> I am nought, I have nought, I desire but only one thing, and that is our Lord Jesus Christ, and to be with him in Jerusalem.

The means to this union with God is the purest prayer we are capable of, and we should not allow ourselves to be held back by sticking to any images or concepts of God which may well be a help to us at earlier stages of our spiritual development. So he accepts the value of vocal and mental prayer, routes into prayer which were described in Chapter One; but he believed that people who gave themselves to prayer would be likely to find them of limited value only, and that they should not be clung to when a person felt a strong impulse to get beyond them to a kind of prayer that is less dependent on words and thoughts, where one puts oneself more simply in the presence of God who may still be only very dimly perceived. Baker accepted that prayer was very much the work of the Spirit in a person's heart, and that it was possible to be too schematic and prescriptive in describing the spiritual course a person might be led by God to follow. 'Follow your call: it is all in all' was one of his catchphrases.

But in his way of presenting the path of prayer, he suggested that people would generally reach a point where systematic meditation was uncongenial, and he recognized that this distaste would occur not because of a lack of spiritual motive but precisely as a result of its development. At this point he advised a person to move on to a freer kind of affective prayer, simply turning the mind and heart to God in various ways such as in thanksgiving, or contrition or self-offering. To start with he recommended the use of set verses or short prayers, such as people might gather from their reading of scripture or the Psalms. He called this kind of prayer, rather unattractively, the Prayer of Acts.

In early editions of *Holy Wisdom* a collection of these was published at the end in thematic series so that a person could quietly repeat them to themselves and use them as a way of renewing the impulse of wanting God, but anyone could make a note of favourites from their own reading. The tradition here goes back to John Cassian and the *Cloud of Unknowing*. One way to encourage this kind of prayer is by using the five-finger method described in Chapter Two, taking one or other style of prayer, such as thanksgiving or sorrow, and either with words or leaving them unsaid, expressing yourself thankfully or sorrowfully towards God. Or you can find that words expressing one or other of these styles of prayer come out of the memory, from well-known scripture passages or prayers. This is where the use of liturgical prayer or *lectio divina* can be so helpful, because both encourage a subconscious memorization of Psalms, scripture or prayers – more sometimes than might have been supposed!

Increasingly, by using this kind of stimulus to prayer Baker believed the will and desire would find their natural orientation towards God, and the acts of will would become less explicit and, as he saw it, more spiritual. From here, prayer becomes more a matter of what he called aspirations than conscious willed acts. We learn a kind of spontaneity of expression in our desire for God (with or without words) which becomes more prevalent, and we find ourselves turning to God from our hearts with little or no difficulty beyond the initial settling down, 'getting into the here and now' as I called it in the last chapter. We can even find what may have seemed distractions turning into the stuff of our prayer: a hurtful remark becomes part of our sorrow or intercession, the excitement of seeing friends or some good news becomes thanksgiving and praise. Even the inner noise we can rediscover as disclosing our vulnerability, our longing or a deeper sense of need that teaches us to recognize and cherish our dependence on God and his love for us. And so there develops the overarching shape of a new kind of prayer that reaches out to God from the fibre of our being and the deeper places of our heart.

Beyond this level of attention, he supposed that the work of prayer became increasingly simplified and passive, which does not mean to say a person stops praying, but that he or she is more immediately responsive to the movement of the Spirit in the depths of the heart. I think it is a natural progression in this kind of praying for it to matter much less where the prayer starts from in us, and for the focus to shift more and more towards God. We matter less and less, and God comes to be all in all. Along the way, Baker recognized that there would be times of light and darkness, times of testing and times of encouragement; but he insisted that one should never be distracted by either experience from continuing to seek God and strive for union with him.

Walking by faith

As we continue in the path of prayer we do so more and more by the virtue of faith. By this is meant that more than before we can feel that we are very much in the dark about what is going on in our prayer; or we can doubt that anything is going on, or that we really know what we are doing, let alone that there is any point. It is customary to appeal here to St Paul's distinction that we walk by faith rather than by sight (2 Cor. 5.7). Or, as he says in the First Letter to the Corinthians (13.12):

> For now we see in a mirror darkly, but then we will see face to face; now I know only in part, then I will know fully, even as I have been fully known.

It is not always as dark as this; sometimes we feel we are in the dark, but it is less confusing, and we feel less anxious. There are lighter times too, when we know that prayer is valid even if we have little sense of what to make of things; and times of encouragement, which can be experienced as times of deep peace, of thankfulness and praise. By the same token, we need to bear in mind though, at all times, that we cannot base any judgements on 'how it goes'; we can only persevere in seeking God and in waiting on him, however that may be. In the old days, people spoke of cultivating a kind of indifference to the way prayer affects our feelings. In truth, we must be grateful for the positive times of consolation; and ready to persevere at other times.

Our difficulty is simply that God is beyond our knowing; however much we can know about him, even from the prayerful reading of scripture, it is not God as such; and in prayer we are learning to reach out beyond the scope of our discursive imagination and reasoning to God, pure and simple. So it is inevitably a very confusing experience, as we have to let our normal habits of reasoning loosen their hold on the deeper levels of our mind, and trust that though we do not see God, he is with us and that the Holy Spirit that is poured into our hearts by Jesus is working to bring us to union with the God whom we long for and seek. It is not that we stop using our minds, or that prayer is irrational. But our minds need to be directed by our heart; in prayer it is love and desire, not knowledge, that orientates our awareness.

We pray because we want God and out of love for him. Nonetheless, prayer is also a work of God's grace. We pray because he loves us first, and through it we are able to grow in his love into the image and likeness of God. We become like the one we seek in our prayer. We do so because this kind of prayer helps to purify and to strengthen our hearts. This process is what we need to look at in the next chapter.

Further reading

The works of the English mystics mentioned in this chapter have been published in many editions. Modern editions of Baker's original texts are being published by *Analecta Carthusiana* (University of Salzburg).

Cloud of Unknowing and other Works, trans. A. C. Spearing (London, Penguin Classics, 2001)

Julian of Norwich, *Revelations of Divine Love*, trans. E. Spearing with an Introduction by A. C. Spearing (London, Penguin Classics, 1998)

Walter Hilton, *Scale of Perfection* (Classics of Western Spirituality) trans. J. Doward Clark and R. Dorward (New York, Paulist Press, 1991)

Augustine Baker, *Holy Wisdom*, ed. Gerard Sitwell (Wheathampstead, A. Clark Books, 1972)

Some modern books are:

Leonard S. Boase, *The Prayer of Faith* (Chicago, Loyola Press, 1987)

Basil Christopher Butler, *Prayer, an Adventure in Living* (London, Catholic Truth Society, 1983)

John Chapman, *Spiritual Letters*, ed. R. Hudleston with an Introduction by S. Moore (London, Continuum, 2003)

Heart of silence

4

Once we have learnt to listen and are getting used to silence, we are on the way to discovering that silence is a deeply creative thing. Saint Ignatius of Antioch wrote in his *Letter to the Ephesians* (Chapter 15)

It is better to be silent and to be (to exist) than speak and have an unreal existence. It is a fine thing to teach, so long as the speaker practises what he preaches. Well there is one teacher – he who spoke and it came to be – and what he did in silence is worthy of the Father. The person who has got a hold on the word of Jesus is, in fact, able to listen even to his silence, so that he is perfect, and so that he lives out what he says, and through his silence is recognized for what he is. Nothing is hidden from the Lord, and even the secret place of our heart is close to him.

The silence we keep in prayer, therefore, helps us to draw nearer to the fullness of life, and the way God speaks his word is by keeping silent. Silence is an extraordinarily creative thing, and we need silence to give God's word space to bear fruit in our lives. It is a school of prayer where we learn to pray in the Spirit which Christ pours out in our hearts (Rom. 5.5).

A seminal book that helped me begin to understand how silence was an experience of God was one by a Carthusian monk, *They Speak by Silences*.

> It is in that depth (of silence) that the Eternal Word is born for each one of us. There lies our whole vocation: to listen to him who generates the Word and to live thereby. The Word proceeds from Silence, and we strive to find him in his source. This is because the silence here in question is not a void or a negation but, on the contrary, Being at its fullest and most fruitful plenitude. That is why it generates; and that is why we keep silent. (p. 5)

School of silence

The Bible gives us a number of pictures that can help us understand this. There are three that come to mind. The first, already implicit in the excerpt from St Ignatius, is the silence of creation itself, the silence before anything came to be. In the silence, however, the Holy Spirit hovers over the abyss, nurturing the chaos in response to God's word, as a hen nurtures her eggs, into creation! In this case, silence is the setting for divine creativity; and it expresses our existential relationship to God as Creator and Father.

The second addresses our sense of alienation from God, our sin and our need for redemption. The most striking image of silence here is the picture of our Lord's silence in his passion, which is drawn from the prophecy of Isaiah: 'Ill-treated and afflicted, he never opened his mouth; like a lamb led to the slaughter-house, like a sheep before its shearers, he never opened his mouth' (Isa. 53.7). The Gospel accounts of the Passion of the Lord recapture the pathos of this vulnerability in describing his silence before his accusers. Christian tradition has meditated on the seven words from the Cross because of the silence of his suffering out of which they were uttered. And the moment of death marks his final return to silence, when he 'breathed his last' and surrendered his spirit to the Father. They are all the more poignant in the Gospels for the fact that each gives only one or two statements. Jesus was the Word of God; he preached a gospel to people like us, but God completed the work of our salvation in silence.

Finally there is the silence of new creation. We do not think of God's conclusion of history as described in the Apocalypse as a quiet affair. But it is easy to overlook an important moment. The author describes how the Lamb who was slain is found worthy to open the Book of Life with its seven seals. It is the opening of this book that unleashes the final acts of the drama of salvation history. The Lamb then broke the seventh seal, and then, before the trumpets sound, there was silence in heaven for about half an hour (Rev. 8.1).

God created, then, out of silence. In silence, the Son of God suffered and died for our salvation. Silence is how God speaks his word, both his creative and his redemptive word; and if we are looking for the new heaven and earth God is creating, we have got to let God speak; and for us to tune into his word, we have got to live with his silence. The new heavens and the new earth come into existence through our allowing our lives to express that word. That means letting God bring his word to birth in our hearts. That means allowing ourselves to enter into the real silence, the silence of God's love and mercy.

It is easy to romanticize about silence, about its saying more than words, about a communion beyond mere words. That's all very well. But to go on like this runs the danger of reducing the experience of prayer to the human level again, a cosy relationship, and of trying to turn God into a romantic object. We forget that Job was reduced to silence before the majesty of God and repented in dust and ashes (Job 42.6). We need to learn that the famous verse in the Psalms, 'Be still and know that I am God' (Ps. 46.10), is not to be cooed, as so often it is in the modern liturgical song: it is the defiant voice of God shouting in triumph over anyone who has the nerve to think they can stand up against him! God's word can be a devastating thing for anything that stands in the way of God's work, if we listen to it. Perhaps it is better he stays silent and that we hear him, as Elijah discovered, not in the earthquake, wind or fire, but in the sound of stillness, 'the sound of sheer silence' (1 Kgs 19.12).

Keeping silence teaches us gradually to get rid of idols, and all our ideas of God that so easily turn into them. We need that kind of space to learn to want God as he is in himself, and nothing less than that. But silence is also something that happens to us, a gift, something we keep holy. In the end we realize this is much more important; it is something we are drawn into. We cannot know God, and we need to be content with that; we can only be known fully by him (cf. 1 Cor. 13.12), and we need to take encouragement and confidence from that. We are always in his sight, but him we do not see. But, as the First Letter of John says (1 Jn 3.2), we hope that in the end we shall see him as he is because we have learnt to love as he has loved us and in that love have become like him (1 Jn 4.17-19). Silently we need to learn that his regard for us is love, a blessing not a threat. Only by being quiet do we learn not to panic – and want nothing less than God. In this God-given silence, God can take the initiative with us and draw us to himself, into the life of the Trinity.

Spirit of prayer

Silence introduces us to our inwardness, to what is often called the spiritual dimension of our life. We know that our life belongs not only to this world we see and feel, the world outside us, a world of change and, for the most part, of decay. We also belong, so long as we are in our mortal bodies, to a world we cannot see, to a world where things do not pass away. This is the dimension of life in which we discover the Spirit. The Spirit is not just inside us; as Jesus says, the Spirit blows where it wills (Jn 3.8), and reaches from the depths of creation to the heart of God (1 Cor. 2.10). But we begin to discover the world of the Spirit only within ourselves, because it is by coming into contact with the Spirit who dwells in our hearts that we develop our awareness of it.

The Spirit is something we desperately need to re-discover. Life is not just biological; the mind is not just material. We are body, mind and spirit: our bodies need food and exercise to flourish; our minds are fed by truth, goodness and beauty, and they need education to flourish. Our spirits also need nourishing. This nourishment comes from the Holy Spirit and from our contact with holiness in all its forms. Conversely, if we lose touch with the sacred, we lose touch with our inmost selves. Prayer attends to this world of the Spirit; we cultivate our awareness of the Spirit by attending to our experience of beauty, truth and good-ness. For the Spirit is the dimension that gives these values their absolute and infinite claim on us. This awareness of limitlessness, of absoluteness and unconditional demand on us is the basis of prayer as an experience of God.

This world is, however, a disrupted world. For there is a critical tension between the Holy Spirit and the spirit of this world, in the sense of a world opposed to God. These

81

two force-fields, as it were, govern two spiritual cultures of good and evil – though really they are a culture and an anti-culture – and the struggle between them runs through our very selves. We have no choice about belonging to the world of the spirit: the question is how we are going to let these two powers govern us. The major obstacle to growth in prayer, once we engage in the effort of prayer, is our loyalty to the spirit of this world and to sin. Brute sin is obviously in direct conflict with the Holy Spirit; but for someone who sincerely tries to pray, brute sin is not usually so much of an obstacle as our loyalty to the sorts of attitudes that give rise to it. These make us careless and inattentive to promoting the life of the Spirit.

These worldly attitudes hang in the air like smells, both distasteful and alluring, while prayer thrives in the freshness of air and the fragrance of soil after a shower. The challenge for anyone who prays is accepting the personal implications of developing an instinct for that 'smell' of the Spirit. For it implies the need to engage in the struggle between good and evil, and of confronting our habits of laziness when it comes to holding fast to what is good, true and noble. But there is also the promise that prayer holds out to us. For prayer helps us flourish as free, human and spiritual beings. Only prayer can heal us from the bruises of a life-and-death struggle with the power of evil. Prayer keeps us upright in the torment and confusion of the world. It helps us redeem the world and make it a place where the Holy Spirit can thrive in the hearts of all.

Praying in Christ

For all the challenges silence presents in prayer, it teaches us that prayer is essentially God's gift. Prayer is the gift of the

Spirit which Jesus pours out in our hearts. The Spirit does not just draw us into companionship with Jesus. As we learn from St Paul (Romans 8), the Spirit is also central to Jesus' own relationship to the Father, and so prayer in the Spirit also expresses our union with Christ as members of his Body, able to turn to the Father and say, as Jesus said, *Abba*, Father. And in this way we discover the completeness of the union to which we are called in Jesus Christ, by our baptism which makes us members of his Body in more than just a metaphorical sense. For in the prayerful movement of the Spirit we come to share in the loving exchange of life that unites the Father and the Son. This is not a permanently comforting or peaceful state; it is often disorientating. For as responsible agents we need to be de-centred and re-centred on him, and not on ourselves. In prayer we discover ourselves, our consciousness, will and love rediscovered as received from him.

This is what makes Christian prayer different. It is not just about our relationship to the source of existence, an existential experience of our human createdness, what I called our Godwardness at the start of this book. Rather, it is the discovery that this orientation and inwardness has a particular shape and structure, which is defined for us by our knowledge of Jesus Christ, and the knowledge of the Father we have through faith in him. To use a modern expression, Jesus 'frames' and 'models' a completely new style of Godwardness, in which we pray to God not as a reality over against us at a distance, but one in whom we discover ourselves sharing a new life, the life of Christ himself.

This is what the disciples discovered in Christ, and what the early Christian writings about the Passion and Resurrection explore in terms of a new access to the Father, a new realization of the Fatherhood of God in the Sonship of Jesus – a Sonship he shares with us in the power of the Holy Spirit. We make this our own by our faith in him, our hope and love. In Christ we grow to our full stature in the image and likeness of God (Eph. 3.8-19).

The Trinitarian shape of prayer

In the end prayer is about opening our hearts to the reality of the divine life of which we are made sharers by grace. It is worship of the Trinity as the source, shape and goal of our lives of faith, a mystery before whom we can only be silent, but also a mystery of our own lives of faith; as St Paul says, we are already being built up in Christ to the full stature of his nature. This is the context in which we ought to talk about contemplation. Contemplation is often talked of as if it were a rather rarefied thing, and a rare gift given to a few saints. Or, as it is often thought of nowadays, it is little more than a fancy word for silent prayer, without any particular theological content. But if we think of it in the perspective of faith that we find in St Paul or St John, as the divine mystery to which we belong and which is progressively unfolding in our lives as we grow in faith and our lives more closely model the life of Christ in the Spirit, prayer can in fact be seen simply as the interior working of that life of faith, and so contemplation is our increasing appreciation in love, joy and hope of the threefold dimension of divine life to which the Spirit introduces us. It is our wonder at the mystery of life on which we depend but which always transcends our understanding and experience.

Knowledge, as Aristotle says at the opening of the *Metaphysics*, starts from wonder. It makes us take an interest in things, makes us ask questions and think. And it is in wonder that we open our minds to the mystery of God. There are, I think, three kinds of wondering which are relevant to knowing God, and to understanding the contemplative character of prayer. Silence gives us the space we need to learn to open our minds in this way to God, the Trinity.

The first kind of wonder is one with which everyone should be familiar. A vivid experience of it for me was as a boy walking home in the snow one night with the sky filled with stars. It is an exceedingly common experience; but perhaps we do not let ourselves wonder at it fully. You can almost touch the stars, and yet they are so far away. The sense of greatness of it all that makes you feel small, yet part of something immeasurably huge, something incredibly wonderful. The sheer fact of the existence of anything at all, the existence of all this – this is, I think, simply wonderful. Even with all the horrors which mar our experience of life, I find it impossible to conceive of the beauty and goodness which clearly is part of life, except that goodness and beauty be the ultimate truth of everything. I can make best sense of evil as a corruption of the way it all should be; but to envisage goodness as part of a grand deception (even a self-deception) in an ultimately evil world, I have to say simply does not ring true to my experience. So I think that the goodness of the world is more fundamental than the evil in it. Nor can I really understand my experience as of a morally neutral world in which some things happen to be good and other things happen to be evil. Wonder is of something real 'out there'; it cannot be only a comment on my way of feeling.

The so-called cosmological argument we find in St Thomas Aquinas takes up this line of thought. The sheer fact of the existence of anything at all, let alone the existence of all this – perhaps we can sum up this kind of wonder in the question 'why all this?' which can be asked as a debating point. But it can also be asked in prayer. The experience of wonder, our sense it is good to be alive, however it arises, can be the start of an experience of God. It opens the mind up to acknowledge a creator. Aquinas concludes *hoc omnes dicunt deum*: wondering taken to a reasoned conclusion. What happens if you stick with the wondering itself? Can we, as St Augustine did, learn to 'turn the light around'? Can we let it open up our awareness to God himself? There is here, I believe, a mystical dimension implicit in our awareness.

This is an ancient line of thinking about mysticism. But I think it goes rather further than this. Another kind of wondering we are all familiar with, certainly in our earlier years, is a kind of wondering I have about myself. But it is one we feel more as anxiety than wonder. It emerges, I suppose, as we try to find ourselves outside the basic security of our home and family, when we have to fit in with others; it could be anybody with whom by chance we find ourselves. This wonder can be spelled out in the simple question 'Am I OK?' which is more profoundly existential than in the title of the popular book on transactional psychology. I can wonder at the sheer existence of everything else, but when I turn that awareness to myself it feels very different. I feel vulnerable. There's no arguing with the existence of other things. They are just there. They simply are what they are. But I do not think I feel the same about myself. I feel the need for some kind of justification, some affirmation that I am OK, and not just because of anything I can do, but just because I am. The despair which seems to lurk in the back of people's minds and which makes depression such a widespread disease among people today (particularly young people) is perhaps attributable to this need for deep affirmation of their need to be themselves.

The typical way we seem to respond to this discomfort is to stop being ourselves, and start trying to be just the same as enough people to make us feel secure. In contrast to the sense of transcendence we get gazing at the stars, here we wake up to the depressing sense of being trapped. We are limited by dimensions which are perhaps characterized as shame at feeling different and its close companion, envy. They generate self-doubt, and unease with one's self even if it is not yet self-hatred.

I suppose that this kind of wondering is fundamental to the consciousness of every human being, but I think it is particularly forceful in adolescence. It is part of the sense of a loss of innocence which happens when we take our first steps towards being selves and which will take us on the sometimes tortuous path to maturity. But people, young and old, devote enormous efforts to trying to be OK, and the anxiety expressed in this question goes deeper than our ability to affirm ourselves or our ability to affirm each other. It is, I am sure, tied up with our consciousness of the power of death over human life. Faced with the reality of death, it is very easy to go for anything which might make me feel OK, and go for it quick, before anyone else can get it, or get more than anyone else can get. At once we are in that world of greed, selfishness and rivalry unto death – a Hobbesian world – which is the world in which sin thrives. 'Who can show me that I am OK?' means in the end 'Can anyone show me that death no longer has the last say?' The second kind of wonder expresses our felt need for justification.

But a third source of wonder arises from our capacity to change and grow to a fullness of life and to give ourselves to others in love. When I was School Chaplain taking Confirmation classes, a recurring question was why it was so much easier to be bad than good! In spite of that, I can change for the better as well as for the worse. But becoming a better person involves far more than I am capable of by myself. What is it that takes me out of myself, or that inspires me to live more fully? And when I consider the world, my sense of responsibility for it and common concern for others, the sympathy I feel for their needs, what does all this mean? Where does my conviction that there is a possible better world come from, and my sense of duty to do my best to realize it?

The source of wonder here is at the possibility of change, of renewal and growth. It is the wonder I discover when I fall in love, the wonder I feel when I discover there is something between me and another person but which unites us in such a way that there is more than just the two of us together. In this experience of wonder, something new has begun to be born, a new world in which everything is different. C. S. Lewis' *Surprised by Joy* gives a fine description of the experience, even in its title. Falling in love is only an extreme case; the same kind of wonder arises, if only we notice it, whenever we find ourselves changed by someone, taken out of ourselves and introduced to a newer, fuller life. A prayer card I am very fond of has these words of Sister Wendy Beckett: 'Expect lovely things of people and they will grow.' That's just right. The people who inspire us are not only those who have a vision to persuade our minds, but people who enable us to believe in ourselves: whose faith in us releases a new source of energy to live as we never could from our own selves.

These kinds of wondering are, to my mind, basic to human experience and they seem to me to open up three dimensions of spiritual awareness as an awareness of the threefold nature of God. They spell out the coordinates of the kind of space we can begin to explore best of all in the silence of prayer. It is a space whose dimensions are those of the Trinitarian God, who discloses himself to us in silence as Father, the source of the existence of all things; Son, the one who affirms my right to be myself, the one who forgives me, heals me, frees me from the power of death – the one who justifies me; Spirit, the source of transformation and new life. As Christians these are the dimensions of the spiritual world within which we move as we make our journey of prayer to our hearts.

We are wrong to expect anything easy or cosy about the Prayer of Silence. Silence will be God's way of exposing what we often try to conceal by talking and being busy; it will bring all our nervousness and anxiety to the surface. This is part of the 'grounding' which I said is so important a part of praying. It is all part of the way God has of teaching us to wait, of trying to let us deepen our readiness and longing for something greater than anything in our puny world of action and language. But when we learn to listen to silence we realize we are tuning into a new way of communicating with God. We are learning a new language of mutual presence rather than of words. It is the way the Father and the Son are present to each other in the Holy Spirit. Silence becomes now a way of praying, a way of letting God pray in us. For us it is also a creative thing because it reverences the space needed for God to change us, to perfect the image of Christ in us and pour out his Holy Spirit in our hearts. It is how we grow in his grace to the full stature of Christ and share more fully in the life of the Holy Spirit.

Further reading

A Carthusian, *They Speak by Silences* (Leominster, Gracewing, 2006)

There are now several similar paperbacks of Carthusian writings readily available:

A Carthusian, *The Prayer of Love and Silence* (Leominster, Gracewing, 2006)
Id., *Interior Prayer* (Leominster, Gracewing, 2006)

Finding
our way

5

Feelings and the thoughts of the heart

Ausgustine – recreating our consciousness,
will and love

Shift from ego to self

We not only need silence in order to pray: it is itself a way of prayer; and silence can become a new kind of language for prayer. Not that we no longer need to use words or ideas, but they are no longer the only way we can pray; often they will serve only to keep our minds occupied while the prayer goes on at a deeper level; and at times they can be an obstacle to our prayer and should be dropped. Once we learn that the prayer of silence is something we receive and that the Holy Spirit is the principal agent, as it were, of God's prayer in us, we will readily see that what we have to do is, as far and as fully as possible, to let the Holy Spirit 'do his thing'.

To do this, we need to reflect on the process of trans-formation at a human level, which is something we can really only do for ourselves. That is to say we need to learn to tell our lives as a story of faith. Prayer has a biog-raphical context. There are various ways in which the process of spiritual growth can be described. In this chapter I will consider three ways. First, there is the ancient monastic idea of the purification of the heart; second, drawing on St Augustine, the idea of an ascent of the mind to God; third, using a more modern psycholog-ical model, the idea of a move from our 'ego' to our (true) 'self'. Each approach offers a map to help us describe the journey we each have to make in our way across the spiritual landscape. However, no book can predict the route we will follow.

Feelings and the thoughts of the heart

The first map describes prayer as a journey that passes from the mind to the heart. It is particularly dear to the Orthodox tradition of prayer, it has utterly biblical roots in the idea of purity of heart and singlemindedness. In the Bible, the heart represents the very centre of the person, where we are most truly ourselves and most immediately present to God our creator, who breathes into us the breath of life. In the New Testament, Jesus uses the image of the inner chamber where we are seen by our heavenly Father. The heart is the source of our deepest acts of thought and will. It is a bit of a cliché to say that the longest journey we ever make is the journey from mind to heart! But there is some truth in it. In prayer, as in the whole of our lives of faith, the kind of knowing that is called for imposes a considerable moral demand. It is a long process learning the integrity and selflessness we need to know God and love him, let alone to serve him and find in him our joy.

Very briefly the journey goes like this. We start with vocal prayer, but if we are really going to pray we also have to mean the words. In doing so we do not just utter them on our lips, we take them into our minds. By doing so, we make the words of others our own and learn from them how to express ourselves in prayer. Prayers like these teach us a language with which we begin to share our lives and concerns with God. This will seem to be largely at the level of our minds, but we do not have to think about it long to realize that prayers express our feelings and desires too. Prayer is naturally a thing of the heart. So it should not be surprising that in prayer words become less important, or that our feelings and desires loom larger. And in this process we should not be surprised that the centre of gravity in our praying begins to shift. Prayer is likely to become much less discursive and thought out in our minds; it is more likely to become a silent, or at least rather inarticulate state in which we are more aware of feeling empty, of wanting, and an underlying desire – without, however, being very clear about what we want or desire, except that nothing in particular will really do.

But there is a much broader, interior landscape across which this kind of journey has to be made. In the earliest monastic writings from the Egyptian desert, monks recognized that, as prayer becomes more and more rooted in the heart, we have to attend to all sorts of trains of thought which pull us away from mindfulness of God and from the source of life in the Spirit. Another monastic metaphor for dealing with this was 'working the soil of the heart'. It is a very good metaphor, with its suggestion of the labour of clearing the stones, digging and manuring. We have stony hearts, and the great clods of earth need breaking up and raking. It can be a heartbreaking business. The early monks thought of tears as a spiritual gift, watering the soil of the heart so that new life could spring from the earth. If tears do not come so easily, we will often feel a heartache, or an inner pang: it is what the monks used to call compunction. It is part of God's process of cultivating the ground, making it fertile. The monks believed that it was important patiently to face up to all this stuff, and to try to let go of it by re-centring and refocusing the mind on God. They believed that this was how God purified our hearts so that we become much more straightforward integrated human beings, and able to see God.

Fundamental to all this are the two ideas, that we are

made in the image and likeness of God, and that this image and likeness are perfectly revealed in Christ. As we grow in purity of heart, they believed, we become more transparent to God's grace, and more closely reflect that likeness; we become like Christ, and grow to our full stature in him. There was an ancient argument as to whether the image was in the soul or in the integral human being; that is not the point here. Either way, it is in our heart that we recognize the fact that we are in God's image because that is the seat of our awareness. It is where we are aware of God dwelling within us through the Holy Spirit. The more like Christ we become, the more conscious we become of that relationship he had with the Father in the Spirit.

Ausgustine – recreating our consciousness, will and love

Another way of looking at the spiritual journey is suggested by St Augustine, who felt that we discover the image of God in our souls, where, deep down, we keep a memory or recollection of God, which is a sign of his continual presence to our minds. This recollection is the basis of our desire, which is infinite in its reach. He expressed it in a prayer at the start of his best-loved work, the *Confessions*:

> O Lord you have made us for yourself and our hearts are restless until they rest in you. (*Confessions* I.1)

For Augustine the difficulty in prayer seems to be (and in this he stands in contrast to the Egyptian monks) not so much the need to purify the heart as to recognize the true orientation of its desire. For Augustine, our restless hearts are basically set on God. He understood that otherwise we would not exist. But we make so many mistakes about the truth of things and about what really matters, and we end up all over the place rather than in the one place where we are truly ourselves and can know God as he really is. As he reaches the end of his search in the *Confessions* he describes his situation like this:

> Late have I loved you, O beauty so ancient and so new; late have I loved you! For behold you were within me and I outside; and I sought you outside and in my unloveliness fell upon those lovely things that you have made. You were with me and I was not with you. I was kept from you by those things, yet had they not been in you they would not have been at all. (*Confessions* X.27)

The underlying discipline of prayer therefore means avoiding the distractions that pull us away from directing our attention inwards and upwards where, in faith and hope, we can find God. The way he describes prayer in the *Confessions* (and much of the text is actually cast in the form of an extended prayer narrative), Augustine thinks of it not just as a search for God and a longing for him, but also as a discovery of him in our human awareness. The outlines of the same ideas can be found in his later work, although by then he seems to appreciate more deeply how elusive this discovery of God is, given his incomprehensibility. But it is also important to say that he thinks of the interior journey not as one to find God, but as one where we simply centre our whole experience, lives and commitments on God. Augustine understands as well as anyone, I think, how relationships, especially those in a religious community, provide a necessary context for Christian life lived to the full. Prayer helps us reach out to others, and to do so with a more Christ-like love.

Augustine's understanding of prayer is part of a much broader and profound mystical theology, and much of the interest in this focuses on the key passages that occur in the *Confessions* that describe this discovery of God. Before looking at them, however, we have to appreciate the biographical context which Augustine believes leads us towards this discovery of God. Augustine does it by telling the story of his life as a kind of interior biography, told as a kind of dialogue, in the form of prayer permeated by the Psalms and other scriptures that he uses to meditate on his own story in the light of God's grace. By 'confession' Augustine means a number of things. He certainly includes the confession of sins. But, in a way more important than that, he means an appreciation of God's mercy and loving-kindness, whose ways he can begin to trace in his life, as well as the confession of praise, celebrating God's glory and goodness to whom he is able at last to return in faith.

We can learn from this that the process of spiritual rebirth for all of us involves a similar process of recollection and story-telling. Like Augustine we need to learn to tell the story of our lives Godwards. Instead of just living it as it comes, and wandering further and further away from God as a result, we need to bring ourselves back to him by finding the way God has been at work in the background and texture of our lives, and telling the story now in a different kind of way, as a story of grace.

This approach to the spiritual life teaches a number of lessons. Augustine saw prayer fundamentally as desire. That is how he felt we could put into effect St Paul's precept to pray at all times, because whatever we are doing our lives can express a desire for God. He also held the view, which is a help to anyone who finds prayer difficult or impossible, that even the desire for prayer is prayer, because it expresses in its own way our desire for God. The important thing is to discover the true reach of our heart's desire. It is not surprising we make many mistakes about this, but we can learn to make better judgements and find the truth thanks to the very nature of our souls as able to know and want the truth.

This is a lifetime's work. It involves a recovery of our whole lives and a reorientation of our way of looking at them and living them. In other works, such as the *City of God* or the treatise *On the Trinity*, Augustine explores this on the vast canvasses of history and metaphysics. The recovery involves our memories and consciousness, our will and our love. The path may initially be described as a journey inwards, but it does not mean turning our back on anything. It is to discover the order to everything, an order rooted in God's own nature as love. It is a renewal of our ability to harness our love and desire for what is truly good and, in so doing, to be able to live in common with others.

At the heart of the process all along is God, who is present to our minds though unrecognized by us. And God is its goal. In his search for God, as Augustine describes it, he reflected comprehensively on everything; it became clear to him that creation speaks of a creator, but could not give him God. 'We are not our own; we are his that made us' (*Confessions* IX.10.25), was the imagined reply of all created things to his question how to find God. The crucial step was to make a turn inwards by returning to his heart. This is not because the world of creation cannot show us God, but because it is only by a reflective process in our minds that we can discover him distinct from other things and therefore learn how to see him in everything. At the critical moment of this discovery, Augustine talks in terms of light, drawing an analogy from the experience of physical vision, but using it now to talk about our understanding of things as a process where we see things with the mind's eye. In order to do so, we see them in and with an intellectual light, the source of which is God. By using this analogy, Augustine articulates his own solidarity with the created order that is the object of his knowledge, as well as the difference between creation and God, who is not only the source of their being, both knower and known, but also the power by which the human being knows reality. God is the light, as it says in the Psalms, by which we see light (Ps. 36.9).

> Nor was it higher than my mind in the sense that oil floats on water or the sky is above the earth; it was exalted because by it I was made. Anyone who knows the truth knows it, and whoever knows it knows eternity. Love knows it. (*Confessions* VII.10.16)

In other words, our acts of mental judgement, where we recognize truth, goodness and beauty in our experience, witness to the fact that the mind has some contact with the source of being and value, in the light of which it makes its judgement. And this is true not only of our reason, but also of our love, our desire for truth, goodness and beauty. God is not someone of whom we are explicitly aware, but we can become aware of him through the process of introspection Augustine describes. What he discovers through this process is not just his own subjectivity as a rational and desiring human being, because the human being's power to know things objectively rests on God's presence to our minds. Only that gives us the subjectivity we need to know anything at all. God's presence to the mind enables me to move beyond a subjective point of view and know the truth. And not just know it, but as lovers of it, to live truthful, good and beautiful lives as well.

The account in the *Confessions* suggests that the goal of the journey of prayer is one whereby we can discover God in our experience as the intellectual light that is in our minds but as a superior and transcendent reality. At its simplest the goal of prayer would be to turn the focus of our attention around, as it were, towards the source of the mind's light. Avoiding the metaphor, this would mean becoming aware of the way in which we are orientated towards truthfulness, or are committed to goodness or attracted by beauty. The return to oneself is crucial to this because Augustine says we live too much on the outside. What he means is we are unable to get beyond the immediacy of this world to move our attention to what is ultimately real. Our experience is morally compromised by the wrong kind of interest we take in things. To some extent the return to oneself is a moral imperative, in order that we can cultivate the right relationship to reality in order to know it fully. A mystical approach to God depends on some measure of asceticism, cultivating ways of living in the truth.

In his later treatise on the Trinity, Augustine develops the ideas of the *Confessions* in some significant ways. One of the developments is the way he explores the relations and interdependence between our memory, our understanding and our will. These famously give an analogy for thinking about the relations between Father, Son and Spirit in the Trinity. But Augustine goes beyond this to show that the threefold pattern of our mental life is grounded metaphysically on God's own nature as Trinity. So he argues that when we remember, understand and want God (or try to do so), our own inner life finds its proper coherence and order. As a result, the image of God that we are called to reflect can be restored – the more perfectly, of course, the more our minds are directed to the things of

God. And in this sense he can say that we are made in the image of God, in our nature as knowers and lovers of God and of the world he has made.

The relationship between love and knowledge is also significant here. Augustine believes that since our existence is grounded in God's goodness, to know God means that we have to embrace the good by love. He certainly accepts that we cannot love what we do not know but he realizes that we can love something or someone as they are in themselves even though our knowledge of them is extremely circumscribed. Accordingly, the path to God will be forged by love, and in order to know God in full, the heart must be reformed by faith, hope and love. This has important implications for the work on which prayer engages us.

The truth that God is beyond our understanding in this life is more deeply embedded in the discussion of this later work, so that our knowledge of him must always be a matter of faith and not sight. In other words, even if we return to ourselves and are able to reach a state of full consciousness of self, there remains a difference between creator and creature that cannot be bridged as simply as it seemed in the descriptions of the ecstasies of the *Confessions* by metaphors of vision. It is not a simple matter of turning inwards and upwards to see the intellectual light above. Creation disrupts the kind of continuum of being which that kind of theory presupposes. It is interesting to see how Augustine found a way forward at that point. We have to look for God in our minds, rather than in the changing world of our material existence, turned from the things of this world and directed to eternal things. In understanding our own intellectual nature as a Trinitarian pattern of memory, understanding and will, we discover ourselves as being in his image; and by the continual turning of our minds and wills towards God our knowledge of him grows by faith.

Augustine still argues that there is a real, albeit mysterious, cognitive relationship between ourselves and God. In the last book of the work, he combines the image of light now with the Pauline image of seeing darkly in a mirror (1 Cor. 13.12). To unpack this metaphor, Augustine draws on the idea of image which plays such a large part in the final book as an explanation of how our relation with God can be understood in cognitive terms. We can see but only indirectly, or, as he puts it, by faith. In the first place, this is because there is more to God than we can ever understand in this life, so that our knowledge of God is always a matter of faith, not of vision. Otherwise we would not continually find ourselves engaged in the search for him. In this life we do not move beyond faith, but faith is a way of knowing God; faith becomes a way to understanding.

The most important lesson I think Augustine teaches is to understand the contemplative aspect of prayer as the discovery of God in our awareness. The mysteriousness of this discovery is one he explores in various works, but central to his theory is the cognitive character of faith, as well as the profound links between the maturing of faith and our moral and spiritual reformation. But if we pay the right kind of attention to beauty, truth and goodness in our experience, we become attuned to these fundamental values and they begin to reshape our lives. Gradually we begin to appreciate that they have an absolute quality to them, which borders on the world of the infinite. This is to begin to turn towards the source of this light. This introduces us into a new atmosphere, the atmosphere of the world of the Spirit, where we enjoy the fellowship of heavenly things, like faith, hope and love.

In our spiritual nature we have an affinity to God. We

should not look straight at the sun, but we are well aware of its warmth and light, and occasionally we get oblique glimpses. Similarly, in this inner world, with God. Prayer attends to the colours and atmosphere of this world of the Spirit; the awareness of limitlessness, of absoluteness and unconditional demand on us is the basis of prayer as an experience of God. Prayer is like trying to turn the mind around to look at the source of the light by which we understand things in terms of their ultimate value.

Shift from ego to self

Those are two different but traditional descriptions of things. Modern psychology too can help give some indications for another map of the spiritual life. Nowadays it is easy to find discussions about psychology and prayer; there's a danger of getting them confused, so that prayer (especially meditation) becomes a therapy for our problems. Prayer always goes deeper than what psychology is primarily concerned with, the *psyche*; for prayer is a matter of attention to God not to that aspect of our inner selves; and, as a spiritual process, prayer goes on at a deeper level than our *psyches*. But there is clearly an overlap of sorts: self-knowledge and truthfulness have traditionally been recognized as fundamental to maturity in prayer, and no less a secure moral sense grounded on goodwill, courage and responsibility. We have all sorts of ways of evading such a sense – especially when it comes to our selfishness, cowardice, and self-indulgence. Perhaps we can say that the spiritual journey to God lies across our *psyche*, and in this sense Jung was right when he called the *psyche* the royal road to the spirit. While we need to distinguish between human and divine in the realm of the spirit, our spirit is the medium through which God, the Holy Spirit, works in our hearts; it is where the Spirit is moving over the waters of the deep.

I can only write on the basis of my own experience and my experience of monastic formation, but some general points seem to me to be worth clarifying. The first is the value of the distinction between 'self' and 'ego', though different terms may actually be used. At its crudest, the 'ego' is that part of ourselves where we interact with others, the 'self' is that deepest part of ourselves that stands in relation to God. The notion of 'part' here is not something that can be separated off from other 'parts' except for the purposes of reflection. The 'self' is where we are in contact with the realm of the spirit, where God touches us creatively and redemptively in his Holy Spirit. The 'ego', on the other hand, is where we live out the life of grace.

It is important to make clear that the 'ego' is where we live out our lives; it is where we are conscious, live and active. We cannot get away from our ego – this is not always clear in what I have read – and we need good egos in order to live out our lives for others. But we need to bring other elements of ourselves into a healthy relationship with it. Above all, we need to change the relationship we have with our 'self' and become aware of the balance between self and ego; the goal of spiritual maturity is to achieve a good level of communication between the 'self' and the 'ego', a kind of transparency between the two.

In practice, I think, the task of spiritual maturity means that we need to tilt the balance in our lives away from the ego so that the self is able to take an increasing role in how we live. For that is the source from which we draw our deepest personal energy, as well as being where we stand before God and where our spirit is animated by the Holy Spirit. More straightforwardly, this means learning not to pursue our own agendas (ego stuff) but instead learning to seek God's will, and make it the centre of our lives. I am sure that saints are people in whom other people can see God, and God is able to work through the saints, because of a high degree of what I call this transparency. An essential part of love is learning to find one's centre outside one's own life.

Conversely, the effect of the tension between the two cultures of the spirit mentioned in the last chapter is one that tends to drive a wedge between the sort of people we really are and the sort of people we try to be, or try to be seen as. So a major element of a spiritual journey will be to address the ways in which the relationship between self and ego has been thrown out of kilter. As a result we can be more or less out of touch with our 'selves' or not, and on this will depend our ability to tune into the way we stand Godwards. We can have 'weak' or 'strong' egos, depending on the way in which (and success with which) we are able to be ourselves in relation to others. Sometimes the challenge of the spiritual life will be to strengthen our egos. It will involve reviewing all sorts of mechanisms, 'defence mechanisms', and trying to enable the ego to be good enough to have a good relationship with the 'self', so that a person can not only relate well with others, but also be 'happy in their skin', as they say, inwardly and can turn towards God in confidence, hope and love.

Because prayer works at the level of the spirit, it inevitably leads to a fundamental shift to a deeper level of existence from the way we normally engage with the world of work and our relationships. It involves a shift in the centre of balance from the 'ego' towards the 'self'. Thomas Merton, for example, spoke of a recovery of the authentic or true self as opposed to all kinds of inauthenticity that disguises human life. This shift in equilibrium loosens up a lot of the pretences and pretensions (connected with the roles we play, our 'persona') as well as the unfinished business of our hurts and fears that we push into the shadow of our unconscious (our 'alter ego'). Not only this, but our deeper (archetypal) needs, attractions and desires begin to make themselves felt in new ways too. Prayer can be very unsettling.

All this can seem a little self-absorbed. But if we are seeking God the attention we give to ourselves is not directed away from God; it's where we are in terms of our orientation towards God, and it is where we find him. Personal stuff becomes the stuff of our prayer, something we can share with him. Once we begin to realize that God, our creator, lets us be even like this, and is ready to listen to all this, we can only learn from his patience and courtesy. He knows and sees us much better than we can see ourselves, and loves us infinitely more than we love ourselves.

The journey of prayer will have some surprises along the way, and be a difficult path to follow; it may feel like a long process of stripping away, or of being turned inside out, before we actually begin to face up to the truth of our selves. In terms of the parable, it is a process by which we unlearn the ways in which we play out the role of the Pharisee and find our real selves in the position of the tax collector (Lk. 18.9-14). But it is a normal process of spiritual recovery and growth for all of us, and however long-drawn-out it turns out to be, it can only be very creative if we engage positively and hopefully with it. In so far as problems are resolved, a more integrated relationship between the various elements of our personality will result: we begin to live more fully, better tuned into our inner resources, better able to live more openly with others. The good news is that it is the process by which we recover ourselves in the true image of God.

Christianity is about self-giving, not about hatred, and not even about self-hatred. So while the work of prayer and the search for holiness calls for radical generosity, it does not mean self-annihilation. Life is essentially a gift we receive. It is given us by parents, and more fundamentally by God. But if life is gift, we can live only by giving. This means learning to live not centred on myself but in relationship to others: God is the fundamental relationship, but increasingly we learn that this relational understanding of myself can exclude no one. I am responsible for everyone in some sense; and contemporary concerns for the environment remind us that we are responsible for every*thing* too. This can certainly call for sacrifices, but when we discover that the risk we take of generosity is met by another's generosity in return, we receive far more than we ever give, because it is shared.

God's love is the truth in which we are here and now created and, therefore, in which we stand before him and can find him. Standing in this truth is more precious than any of the prayers we try making for ourselves. The essential thing in prayer is honesty, and that thoroughgoing honesty which we call integrity, that ability to let all the various parts of our lives speak and listen to each other and turn towards God. This inwardness will be pretty chaotic until we start paying attention to it, but as we do so we can begin to find our way forwards. It is where we find God and that is far more important than anything else going on in our awareness. We can begin to learn that God is listening to us and waiting for us to calm down and tune in to ourselves. As we do so we can begin to learn how we can tune in to him. For we can begin to understand and learn to recognize in ourselves a new language, not of words but the basic language of our life.

Further reading

Augustine of Hippo, *Confessions (Works of Saint Augustine: A Translation for the 21st Century)*, trans. M. Boulding (New York, New City Press; pocket edition, 2001)

Igumen Khariton of Valamo (ed.), *The Art of Prayer: An Orthodox Anthology*, trans. E. Kadloubovsky and E. M. Palmer with an Introduction by Kallistos Ware (London, Faber & Faber, 1997)

St Theophan the Recluse, *The Path of Prayer: Four Sermons on Prayer* (Newbury, MA, Praxis Institute, 1992)

Making peace

6

On the way to God there is a lot of interior work to be done. This work is not just for one's own sake. The achievement of some measure of spiritual integrity is a vital part of the work for reconciliation in our relationships and, more broadly still, for peace in our society. It is not only about the promotion of contemplation; it is also about promoting charity. In psychological terms we could think of this as finding healing and wholeness, the spiritual integrity we need to give ourselves wholly to God and to others. Augustine might think of it in terms of redemption and healing of the memory, as well as a simplification of the will so that a person can love with his or her whole heart. The Egyptian monks would have talked straightforwardly about the purification of the thoughts of our heart.

We need to emphasize this all the more in our culture, which is so driven by programmes, action and targets: contemplative prayer makes a major contribution, and an irreplaceable contribution, to our ability to address the most important challenges facing the world today. At its simplest, we have to learn to be peacemakers. To make peace in the Church and the world, we have to learn to make peace in smaller-scale and ordinary ways in our immediate communities. We can only achieve this by knowing how to make peace in our own hearts.

It is a question of making peace, not of finding it. Peacemaking comes at a cost. It calls for a profound sense of humility and patience. This is something I believe underlies the importance laid in the *Rule of St Benedict* on humility, and as he puts it in the *Rule*, it is something that can only be learnt by a serious commitment to contemplative prayer.

Patience with the windings of the soul

Human lives have a moral and historical texture that the work of promoting as well as growing in holiness cannot ignore.[1] Each of us has to live our lives in relationship with others, with some more closely than with others, whether we are modelling ourselves on them or reacting against them. We never start from scratch. Even before we attain any kind of control over ourselves or are able to make choices of our own, so much of the opening chapter of our story has already been drafted by the stories of those closest to us. And this continues for the rest of our lives, albeit in a more dialectical relationship with them. As Rowan Williams says, all our lives represent our attempt to deal 'with the legacy of lives already lived, decisions made, injuries given and received', both in our own case and in other people's. And more than just a legacy, there are the unresolved issues that also have to work themselves out: we are living with the wreckage of lives half-lived, as Eliot says in *Murder in the Cathedral*, 'living and partly living'.

---

1 I have been greatly influenced here by R. Williams, 'Patience with the windings of the soul', *Church Times* 10 January 1992, excerpted from a chapter in Jeffrey John (ed.), *Living Tradition: Affirming Catholicism in the Anglican Church* (London, Darton, Longman and Todd, 1992).

The aphorism, 'God writes straight on crooked lines', should be a source of encouragement and, as already suggested, one of the key rules of prayer is to let God take his time. Patience is of the essence of contemplative prayer, not really for God's sake, but for ours. To live a life of prayer will mean learning to work together with God's Spirit in changing us so that we can grow to perfection. To labour the metaphor, prayer will include letting so much crumpled-up paper be rescued from the waste-paper bin and smoothed down so that God can start writing his own story of our lives. Contemplative prayer is one of the best ways we have of engaging in this long process.

This is because it is so often in prayer that we have the quality of time and space to become aware of all that is involved in our being who we are at that moment, the moral and historical density of our lives, the compromises we have made, the issues we have avoided in our prevarications with the call to personal growth and spiritual maturity. Prayer is the best environment to accept all this without panicking too much, because of the supportive care we find from knowing we are in God's presence. We can learn from the attention, patience and care that God shows each of us, what Julian of Norwich calls God's courtesy, how to accept and take care of ourselves. This is the necessary first step towards taking responsibility for others.

The cultivation of patience and an attentive love towards others calls for no less tact and courtesy, a readiness to let be. To deploy another aphorism, 'men rush in where angels fear to tread'. We do have a part to play, but we need the wisdom of the Spirit that we learn in contemplative prayer to know how to assist the Spirit rather than just to try to take things over. Healing and reconciliation in the public sphere is facilitated by the transparency of our lives to the life and work of the Spirit.

We can find encouragement, though, in the healing power of the spiritual dimension, and in the natural tendency for living things to heal. Some serious injuries need doctors, careful diagnosis and even hospitals. But the spiritual life is so often a matter of letting things heal; it is not a good thing to scratch and pick at scabs. We only need a sufficient measure of resolution for us to 'move on' – that is the modern jargon – for we do not enter heaven as spiritual athletes, but as ordinary human beings helping each other on the way. Some of us will have crutches; most of us will have bruises and blisters; but walking, limping or running, we depend on others to reach heaven, and others depend on us. 'Bear each other's burdens and so fulfil the law of Christ' (Gal. 6.2).

Purification of hearts

Purity of heart is a very traditional term for what we need to undertake this. Its importance comes from the Gospel Beatitude where Jesus says 'Blessed are the pure in heart; for they shall see God.' In his First Conference, John Cassian was only drawing on monastic tradition when he described purity of heart as the immediate goal of a person's endeavour who was seeking the perfection of the Kingdom of God, and the achievement of it he called con-templation. But it is about the perfection of the Kingdom of God, and it goes further than just contemplation towards the construction of what Stanley Hauerwas called the Peaceable Kingdom. Cassian can sound very unfash-ionable today, even in Christian terms: perfection sounds not only elitist but also a denial of the freedom of God's grace; purity carries the smack either of cultic ritualism or of a moralism that jars with our notions of divine mercy and love. And it probably also still sounds as if it is about sex rather than about our proneness to sin. But monks in the last fifty years have begun to appreciate the close relationship between contemplation and justice (which has environmental as well as social demands), and this should help refresh our appreciation of purity of heart.

Today we are closer to Augustine than Cassian in seeing that our souls are ineluctably compromised with sin and death in this life; that everything depends on God's grace; and that in this life we will never see God. But this puts us in danger of complacency, of feeling that, since it is not for us to attain only by our efforts, we do not need to make any effort to reach the goal. This arises, I think, from misunderstanding the monastic insight about our need for the purification of our hearts to promote contemplation. The point is not that we can be morally or spiritually perfect, but that we need forgiveness. Moreover, to live from God's grace means to live mercifully towards others; and, beyond that, it expresses our confidence that we do have the opportunity in this life to know God, love him and serve him in each other, and find the joy and peace of the Holy Spirit thereby. God is unbounded in his mercy; nothing we do can earn what he gives freely to those who love him and seek him. The challenge of faith is to open our hearts to receive what God wants to give us, and to let the new life of divine grace flourish in our hearts and minds.

This knowledge of our need is how we grow in purity of heart. Older metaphors used to describe contemplation in terms of polishing the window of our heart to let in God's light, or (switching to a picture of the heart as a lake) of letting the waters of our heart fall still so that it can reflect the image of God. It is probably more illuminating to think of contemplation as transparency in the more modern sense, of truthfulness with oneself, both in what we do and say, of truthfulness in the biblical sense of being honest and straight with God in our lives.

It is no easy matter either. It is a matter of untangling our lives or, as Rowan Williams put it in a memorable phrase, of patience with the windings of the soul. It also means carrying a cross and fighting with demons. If this sounds grim, there is peace at the end; and as the Passiontide hymn says, 'the Cross shines forth in mystic glow'. For in the struggle, God makes his presence felt. That is how we can address the fundamental need we have for integrity, to become transparent to God, as well as recover our awareness of God, so that we can see him by faith; or at least so that we can walk in his light and radiate it for others to find the right way.

Hearts in need of healing

At this point we can enlarge on some of what was mentioned in the previous chapter. We are created for God, and our deepest desire should be found in our attraction to him. But we are not properly in tune with our heart; other discordant elements get in the way of our awareness of God and a basic desire or instinct for him. We see how this happens all the time: I want something, becomes I need something, with all the restless and justifying imperatives of need. But real needs are easily obscured, and real desire turns into something much more trivial, almost anything that tickles our fancy, or that just seems to offer the promise of an immediate, if short-term, profit, or just a 'quick fix'.

Failing to deal with these interferences to our true desire, we can only satisfy ourselves with things that are less than God, and which thus become idols that claim our attention rather than God himself. The hold of sin on our lives means that our true desire is disguised and distorted, but also corrupted. The story of the Fall points to this fundamental experience of ourselves as being out of tune, and spiritually uncoordinated; we shy away from the very source of our life, and indeed our habits are not only callous as to the sanctity of life but even self-destructive.

Our hearts need to be recreated. The Bible describes a fundamental change that needs to take place – the need for our hearts of stone to become real hearts of flesh. Ancient monastic tradition saw a positive value in the grief that we can feel, either at what we have done or at the sense of frustration and futility we experience: the tears we shed, even if only metaphorically, help to soften the heart and make it more 'fleshy'. Tears are central to the work of the spiritual life; and they are a gift of the Holy Spirit. The creator of life is its only source of healing and transformation. And this work of healing looms large in the life of prayer. For it is in our times of silent prayer that we try to listen. We are listening to God, but again and again we find ourselves getting in the way in all sorts of different ways. At an earlier stage of this book this sort of thing was described as 'distractions', and the thing then was to try not to let them get in the way too much by paying them any attention. This is by and large true for what could be called external distractions like the noise in the street; and also for much of the flotsam and jetsam of our surface consciousness, the way the day past or to come tries to grab us. Now it is time to draw some distinctions, and to note that there are some trains of thought that need a different approach.

This is because these trains of thought do not come from outside but from within. They may be as articulate as thoughts, or they may be less coherent, more like moods, preoccupations, or obsessions. But they suffocate the spirit. It may be only in prayer that we give ourselves a chance to let the spirit breathe and become aware of them. We are terribly moody creatures; and even in prayer we have to learn to be aware of that – and not let them get in the way of real sharing with God. It is often said therefore that we must pay no attention to feelings in prayer. Prayer is knowing and loving God. It is not a feeling. But we need to find a way through these 'feelings' to reach the heart where we truly can know God and love him.

The early Egyptian monastic tradition found a synthesis in Evagrius, who identified eight such trains of thought (or *logismoi*) characteristic of what gets in our way: gluttony, lust, love of money (and things), anger, dejection or despair, boredom, the numbness of spirit which has the old fashioned name *accidie*, and the listlessness which goes with it, boastful vanity and pride. Evagrius' teaching is reflected in the great work of John Cassian who transmitted it to the Latin monastic world, including St Benedict and St Gregory the Great. From St Gregory derives our list of seven deadly sins, although in their original treatment as trains of thought they are not so much sinful as leaving us vulnerable to temptation and sin because they lead us up a garden path from our real selves into fantasies.

So if we are truly seeking God and strive to turn to him in our hearts, we must pay attention to ourselves, not because we are able to be perfect, but because we are seeking the place of truth in the heart where he can be found. In the prayer of the heart, we will find ourselves looking at what, in all honesty, we do not want to see: all those trains of thought and desire which distract, entrance and finally possess us. But the worst deception is our self-deception; honesty about ourselves helps us to the greater honesty by which we confess the fact that we are not our own, but belong to him who made us, from whom we draw life, being and knowledge.

The way to our heart lies through these thickets, and it is there we may listen to the word of God, which has been planted in us and can save our souls. The truth is in our hearts, which is the 'secret place' where we are seen by our heavenly Father who is in heaven (Mt. 6.6ff.). This place is more profound than our feelings, although our feelings are a way of finding the way there, and it is from the heart that we learn to love God, ourselves and anyone else. If we think of prayer, then, as a journey from the mind to the heart, we will be bound to have to find our path through our emotional lives. But in spite of the romantic myth of love, our emotions are not our heart, which lies beyond them, The good news here is that we should not be afraid of our feelings as such; on the contrary, they mark out for us in some way the path to the heart we have to follow. The mistake we often make, though, is to get distracted and pulled off the road by the way we feel.

Forgiving oneself

Only the God who created us can recreate us. Basically we must let healing come from the Holy Spirit. We ought to be confident that he does heal, because Jesus has poured out the Spirit in our hearts. Faith in Christ's redemption and in his undying love for us enables the love to grow in our hearts that overcomes the power of death and brings us into a new relationship of adoption with the Father of all mercies. Neither ought we to be surprised, when we try to let this new sense of relationship with God unfold and grow in prayer, that other stuff – we may have pushed it away for years – begins slowly but gradually to come to the surface. This may be anything, but it needs to be dealt with prayer-fully; for it is part of ourselves; it may even be quite a big part of ourselves, however much we dislike it and have tried to forget or disown it. The fact that it is coming to light is, I think, normally a sign of grace, because we have to integrate it into ourselves for the Spirit properly to heal it.

In the realm of grace, the Holy Spirit works through our consent and freedom. We need to get prayerfully involved in the work of the Spirit. We do this by learning to know ourselves – to recognize the feelings, accept ourselves and let God touch us. This is a far deeper thing than psychotherapy; it is opening up our deepest selves to the Holy Spirit. I like to think in terms of the way human beings are said to be in the image and likeness of God. Each of us reflects something unique of God himself; and by learning in this way to understand and accept ourselves as whole people, we are recovering the divine image of ourselves and can hope to glimpse something of God.

So when we begin to approach the heart, we must not be surprised if we get a clear sense of all sorts of thoughts and feelings we have tried to ignore or push away from attention in normal life. As this happens, we should try to acknowledge them, even try to put into words how they feel, and let them be there as part of our prayer. But we need to be very gentle with ourselves and try to befriend that side of ourselves we have let sour because we did not like it. We should not be surprised about feeling how angry, or how fearful we really are. We may realize how impure our best intentions are, or that there are some pretty bad intentions lurking around. We will probably begin to feel guilty about all sorts of long-forgotten, little things. We have to be honest. If we are at fault, we must say sorry, make amends. Confession and spiritual accompaniment do have a part to play here. But these are all means; the heart of the process is learning to love and forgive oneself, by learning that God already has.

It is not always a matter of bad feelings! Good feelings can be a help and encouragement: sometimes we need them; and God is merciful; but they can also be a distraction, and they are very, very deceptive. If we pray in order to get nice feelings, a 'high' – or just a sense of peace, we have completely missed the point. We are looking to ourselves, not to God. Bad feelings, on the other hand, can turn out to be more helpful than we think. For it is by repentance that we make progress to God, that we enter the Kingdom of Heaven. Over time I think there will be a shift and we will discover we have learnt to love and forgive ourselves. Conversion is a matter of letting the whole of us slowly turn towards God. Then we can love our neighbour, as Jesus says, as ourselves (Mt. 22.39).

The Psalms give a good example of this sort of thing. They describe, and give vent to, every emotion under the sun. St Athanasius described them in his *Letter to Marcellinus* as a mirror of the soul. Their explicitness is often shocking to those hearing them for the first time. A far cry from prayer, they can seem. Not at all. That is so often how we are; and it is as we are that we have to pray, honestly and humbly. And just as there is often a shift to a moment of reconciliation, so we can hope gradually to work towards that in our prayer. In God's good time.

The journey to the heart takes us through the density of our emotional history and also beyond, to our conscience. We also have to learn on the way that our conscience is one thing, a holy thing; but there is a sense of guilt which is not the conscience, but a man-made thing, which tells us more about the way we have been ticked off by fathers or father figures, and then the way we tick off ourselves (not to mention everybody else), than about God. Conscience is our capacity to know God as the source of goodness and the judge of right and wrong; the other is an idol of what is right and proper; it must be patiently destroyed.

The deep and recurring problem is that we do not like ourselves. I once made this observation to a monk who felt that, on the contrary, we had far too big an opinion of ourselves. But this self-satisfaction is not the same as really liking ourselves. That comes, I think, only from the godly love we need to learn. In actual fact, I think many of us can actually be rather angry about ourselves and what lies behind our self-dislike; but we generally suppress the feeling and get by, living with a quiet but deep sadness instead. It is very common for people who are trying to live a life of prayer to have to address problems with what is popularly called self-esteem. This undermines our ability to live out the virtues of faith, hope and love. More is called for here than the popular psychological literature of positive thinking; sometimes that kind of thinking has been a man-made compensation we need to drop as well! As with other bad feelings, we need to be patient in accepting the truth of this fundamental self-dislike by letting God look at us feeling like that, and realizing he does not condemn us and we certainly do not need to condemn ourselves; instead he actually does like us, and we can afford to make friends with ourselves. 'O God be gracious to us and bless us: let your face shine on us and we shall be saved' (Ps. 67.1).

A different kind of anger poses another kind of problem; this is the problem of justified anger, where we are powerless to act or have been unable to do so. Again, we need to be able to accept the anger as well as the angry part of ourselves as a first step. As we try to pray with the anger, we are actually having to work towards an acceptance of the fact that the world is an unjust world. This is not anyone's fault – however much individuals are in fact to blame – but because it is a finite world. It is compromised by sin as well as one in which human desires, however good and just, can never be fulfilled. Etty Hillesum put it better than anyone else probably can in her wartime diaries, if only because of her courage in facing death together with the rest of her people:

> I really see no other solution than to turn inwards and to root out all the rottenness there. I no longer believe that we can change anything in the world until we have first changed ourselves. And that seems to me to be the only lesson to be learned from this war.

Like Etty Hillesum we need to grow towards a peaceful acceptance of the way all human beings are victims of a world systematically subject to a power of evil that can only be overcome in a totally different kind of way.

Making peace with one's enemy before sundown

This is where we move from learning to make peace in our own hearts to making peace in the world. The starting point is recognizing that whatever the problems other people cause, we are in exactly the same position as they are, and we need to acknowledge our solidarity with them to that extent. Then we may be able to take initiatives in facilitating the desirable changes. It is not that we have no right to judge others, but it is too easy to judge them as though we were not implicated ourselves in the difficulties underlying their faults. It is too easy for us to play the part of Pilate. It is a good way of trying to make ourselves feel better.

Jesus said 'do not judge'. I think the point is not that we

cannot or should not judge, but that it will not really address the problem, which can only be addressed by recognizing our solidarity with others rather than our superiority over them. To be sure, none of us can claim the righteousness needed to 'sort things out' on our own account. And Jesus, the only righteous human being, actually shows us someone whose approach, while including forthright words and actions, was fundamentally the path of solidarity with people who cannot help themselves, even to the extent of accepting the role of innocent victim. This is profoundly paradoxical, but we need to learn from it if we are to understand the truth about peacemaking: peacemaking depends not on an assertion of rights, but on acceptance of solidarity, and the fact that I may be in a position to take initiatives towards change that another person cannot yet make.

Peacemaking involves setting others free to change, and by putting oneself alongside them, by not asserting oneself over them, trying to create the possibility of change in the human relationships that need healing. We cannot make friends with enemies just like that, in one step, but we can love them like that, and by playing out the possibility of friendship, offer them the chance of change. This certainly means taking risks and putting our trust in others. If we take initiatives with trust, we will always find ourselves let down in the end; but life would be unbearable if people did not trust each other. Without it there is no possibility of change.

Peacemaking means restraint in assertion of oneself; but we do have to assert the truth. However, we need to strive for a truth that can be spoken with love and compassion, a truth that is not being used as a weapon in a contest of strength, a truth that subverts the other person's defensiveness (which is what underlies their violence) and gives them a chance to recognize one's own point of view. It does not mean making oneself a mat to be walked over. This calls for real courage, as well as self-sacrifice for the sake of the good of the other person. But it is through such Christ-like responses to wrong that the Spirit of new life can work through us in the hearts of others. It is learning to care for others.

St Benedict on humility

One of the most important chapters in the *Rule of St Benedict* is the chapter on humility (*Rule* 7). Its importance lies, I think, in St Benedict's insight into peacemaking in monastic community life. Elsewhere in the *Rule*, he reminds monks of the wisdom of not letting the sun go down on one's anger, and when a monk thinks that another member of the community is upset because of something, the monk should prostrate himself and beg pardon (*Rule* 71). There is no question here of who is in the right or of what might have prompted the behaviour that has caused the upset. The precept is about taking the initiative in making a different future possible. The chapter on humility is certainly central to Benedict's understanding of monastic wisdom, and I think there is much that can be applied to Christian life as a whole.

St Benedict starts by taking over the gospel principle that people who exalt themselves will be humbled, and people who humble themselves will be exalted (Lk. 14.11; 18.14). It is the same in prayer. Prayer has often been described as raising our hearts and minds to God; but, as with St Benedict's teaching on humility, we go up by going down. We need to grow in humility, and discover our really fundamental need for God. We are nothing without him: in him we live and move and have our being. The New English Bible paraphrased the start of the Beatitudes in Matthew 5, 'Blessed are the poor in spirit', as 'Blessed are they who know their need of God: the Kingdom of Heaven is theirs.' Julian of Norwich taught that Jesus is the ground of our beseeching. Prayer is also in important ways a descent into the ground of our beseeching. We desire God best as we become aware of our need for him.

This is where humility starts. The first step on St Benedict's ladder of humility speaks at length about cultivating a sense of God's presence and a mindfulness of him. For this is the first step towards facilitating transformation. Prayer makes it possible for a human life to be reshaped and as we grow in union with Christ and are more deeply united with his Passion, not only will our lives be transformed but we will be a source of redemption and a channel of new life for those around us. That is the goal. To start with though, we acknowledge we are dust, and in recognizing that we learn to rediscover ourselves as people animated and shaped by God. St Benedict teaches that humility promotes a continual awareness of God; and that the natural fear we have can be changed to love. 'All my desire is before you': and God purifies our desiring.

It is only the start of the journey downwards! An attitude of mindfulness needs to work itself out in practical terms of obedience, which is seen in the broadest sense, in Jesus' words, of 'seeking not my own will, but rather the will of him who sent me'. We need to want what God wants, not what we want, or perhaps better, we need to want because God wants it, not because we want it. As St John of the Cross said, 'In his will is my peace.' In doing so we can become channels of peace.

That is the next step, and it leads to the third and fourth steps, where humility begins to rub. Humility enables service; it gives us the resources to put ourselves out for others, in St Benedict's words, to be obedient in concrete terms to those around us. The most elementary way in which this arises for us is in our readiness to make commitments to others, and above all life commitments, in marriage, religious life or whatever. But Jesus became obedient unto death. For the demand of love is ultimately unlimited. At its simplest, life is a gift, and we learn to live only by making a gift of it. It is not hard to give out of our abundance; we can often expect to receive at least as much in return. Jesus gave his life away as a whole, keeping nothing back for himself. By following this example of radical generosity we are able to experience the redemption of Christ, and share it more widely through our own lives, promoting the transforming life of the Spirit.

And even then our limits will be tested! In the fourth step Benedict develops a line of thought that runs through steps five, six and seven. We will suffer hardships and be unjustly treated. It is a challenging observation for someone embarking on life in a monastic community, but that is the way fallen human nature works itself out in the way we live with others! We take it (and it can be anything) out on each other. If we are really engaged in the work of redemption and the Spirit's power to change, it is a habit we have to stop.

We stop it (over time) by dealing with our 'bad thoughts' in a different way. St Benedict reminds us of our Lord's patience in suffering without resistance. He does not doubt a committed life will give many occasions to feel badly about things, and that we will be afflicted by harmful trains of thought. I think that underlying what he says is the insight that we need to take responsibility for the way we are affected by other people, and rather than play out the role of victim try to discover a more positive strategy of engaging with others, taking initiatives in trying to change the dynamic of relationships in a community. Hence the effort implicit in the middle steps of humility to avoid discontent even in the humblest of circumstances, however justified, and not to assert oneself or project one's own ambitions, but to be indifferent to one's status and deserts. It is a highly paradoxical programme and utterly counter-cultural. It is extreme, but there are circumstances where extreme measures are called for. For it is how we learn to be completely identified with Christ, able to let him live completely in us and through us.

For a monk, this involves his complete identification with the monastic way of life which is implicit in the last steps of St Benedict's ladder of humility. For Christians in general it is an encouragement fully to engage in the communities of which they are part, without counting the cost of discipleship. Even as St Benedict reaches the rock bottom in the downward path, he gives some indications about how to live out this radical humility. 'They are so confident in their expectation of reward from God that they continue joyfully and say, "But in all this we are conquerors because of him who so greatly loved us."' They should acknowledge any bad trains of thought or deeds that they have hidden from themselves, referring to the verse 'Make known your way to the Lord and hope in him.' However badly they feel about themselves, they can always say 'Yet I am with you always.'

The patience that is implicit in St Benedict's discussion of humility is needed in order to promote what has traditionally been called purity of heart, but which can perhaps be understood better nowadays as integrity of life. The cultivation of such integrity of life is not only the precondition for contemplation as, for example, John Cassian understood it; it is also the precondition for the life of charity. For it is a quality of life that most of all promotes the health and spiritual vigour of Christian communities as well as our individual efforts as Christians, so that God can work through us and through them to help bring healing and redemption to the world, and thereby the promise of change and the hope of glory.

This journey of prayer is one which a Christian makes for all, for the salvation of the world. It is not an ego-trip or selfish. The patience we learn to take with ourselves, the measure to which we can allow things to untangle in our own lives, teaches us the discretion and wisdom to listen to, accompany and support others. Learning to make peace with ourselves helps us 'earth' the lack of peace in others. This promotes peace. The spirit of the world, the hold of evil over the world, can only be finally defeated by humankind in human hearts. The only heart to which any of us has real access is our own. But to engage in the struggle is to fight for the freedom and salvation of humankind.

Rowan Williams, in the article I have already cited, sums up what this chapter has been trying to explore:

> Our life in the community of Christ produces a style and a sense of human identity that takes us definitively beyond individualism. We assume all along that we as individuals in isolation do not apprehend the truth. It is in giving and receiving of Christ's loving attention that we become persons who know and who live in truth. And the Catholic Church is in this perspective the Church of catholic persons listening patiently and expectantly to each other and in this exchange being brought towards the truthfulness of Christ (judgement and promise) discovering more deeply the spring of their common life, how the one Christ appears in the real diversity of many lives.
>
> Expecting holiness in one another is not a matter of optimism. It is what we learn by discovering in our-

selves that repentance constantly opens us to an in-exhaustible source of mercy and nurture. We do not come to expect holiness without acknowledging failure and injury, nor can we cope with the full disturbing recognition of our failure and injury without the expectation that God will make us whole if we let God do so.

Further reading

An Interrupted Life: The Diaries and Letters of Etty Hillesum 1941–43, quoted in *Peacemaking Day by Day* (London, Pax Christi, 1990), p. 10.

Ann and Barry Ulanov, *Primary Speech: A Psychology of Prayer* (London, SCM, 1985 / Westminster, John Knox Press, 2007)

Priesthood of prayer

7

Intercession

The Eucharist, the source and
summit of prayer

Much of this book has focused on exploring prayer as an interior journey, seeking God in the depths of our heart. But the contemplation of God is totally different from the contemplation of our navel! We never draw near to God by drawing away from others. We can only draw near to God through the love that unites us to everyone else. God is never separated from his world; prayer is never separated from life. We need to pray for God to enable us to discover the resources of love we need to show others. So the love of God and the love of our neighbour are one and the self-same love. Our journey inwards is only one swing of a pendulum that reaches as far out as well. But it reaches out now in the power of the Spirit with the arms of our Lord and with his compassion and generosity.

In Chapter Four I tried to examine how profoundly prayer unites us in the life of the Trinity, through Jesus Christ, thanks to the gift of the Holy Spirit, which is his gift of prayer. One of the most precious memories of the early disciples that is recorded in the Gospels is the memory of Jesus at prayer. Even Jesus had to pray; and in prayer he learnt how to live for God as well as for others. In the same way prayer opens up for us the sense of being towards God; it is where we discover how to respond with our lives to the word by which God calls us into existence and the invitation he gives us to share in his work of redemption.

Already in the last chapter, we began to consider how prayer helps us engage in the work of reconciliation and peacemaking, and it is with this that I want to continue in this chapter by reflecting on the idea of prayer as a way of sharing in the priesthood of Christ.

St Paul described a priest as someone who acts as a mediator between God and humankind (1 Tim. 2.5). It is as a human being that Jesus is priest and the one who has worked our redemption (Heb. 4.14–5.3). And it is as human beings that we share in that work of redemption through him. There is no distance between God and the world – from God's point of view. But most people feel, and in their hearts and lives are, a great distance from God. The Latin word for priest, *pontifex*, means bridge-builder; and in a real sense, priests are called to bridge gaps and become points of contact with God for people of all sorts and to open up paths for them to come to God.

The Second Vatican Council applied these ideas to every Christian when it said in the decree on the Church, *Lumen Gentium*, that by baptism all Christians share in the work of Christ as prophet, priest and king. As prophets, all baptized people are called to witness to the values of the gospel, to speak out in its name but especially to witness by the example of their lives. As kings, we are called to exercise authority and dominion in our respective areas of competence, but following the example of Christ who made himself last of all and the servant of all. As priests, we join Christ in his work of consecrating the world by our lives of faith in family and working lives. Service and self-sacrifice are part of Christ's priesthood. Prayer is another. This is how Jesus taught us the meaning of his life, the way we were to fulfil his command to love each other, in our humble service of each other. He was able to complete his Father's will because he prayed. John 17 gives us Jesus' prayer after the Last Supper for the disciples and for all who through their word believe in him. The other Gospels show us Jesus at prayer in the more anguished setting of Gethsemane where he knelt simply before the face of his Father. Prayer and service are the two hands of Christ's priesthood by which the world is saved.

Two ways in which prayer is a way of living out the priesthood of Christ are by praying for others and by offering ourselves to God to be, according to his will, part of the answer to prayer. As we grow in prayer I think we learn how closely intercession and offering ourselves for the service of others are closely intertwined; both work together to express the depth of our concern for others, which ought to broaden and deepen in its range as we come to a deeper sense of our identity in Christ and of the life of the Spirit in our hearts that draws us into prayer. It is right that we should share Christ's sense of responsibility for others as well as his commitment to them, not to replace the redeeming power of Christ but to enable it to be a living source of hope and new life in the world through us. Of course we do not do this alone but in Christ with the rest of the Church. This brings us to the Eucharist, which is the supreme form of Christian prayer, and forms a fitting conclusion to this book.

Intercession

There's nothing wrong with asking God for things; it is the most straightforward way we learn to pray. But intercession in its proper sense must deepen to become more than just a shopping list of good causes and good intentions. As prayer shifts to the deeper level we have been thinking about in this book, we learn to more interested in God than in what we want: we learn to pay attention to him, to get absorbed in him. Here begins the path of purification and simplification which takes us to our hearts. This new context for prayer, in which we begin to identify with God's own life, goes on in our hearts through the Holy Spirit, and it deepens our awareness of God as well as of ourselves and our need for him. This is bound to lead us to pray for others in a different way, to seek only for God's will, to love it and find our fulfilment in doing it.

Prayer should teach us a new outlook on everything, and we could call this learning to see things from God's point of view. That must help us become a little less selfish about our ideas of what we should pray for, more aware of what God sees in someone, and it should also help us want what God wants for the person in a particular situation. Prayer should encourage an expansion of our sympathies and increase the charity with which we can pray for others.

Intercession is a sign of love. It not only expresses our concern about others, but it is also a proof of God's love for them in Christ. The difficulty is that our hearts are narrow; but the poverty of love, which is all we can ever express in our prayer, is love that God can transform. He takes our human love and turns it into a vehicle of his divine love. This is how we come to share in the priestly intercession of Christ. To intercede for people with God really means to bear them before God in the love of Christ. The more closely we are united with Christ, the more profoundly will we enter into his prayer for all people, and the more palpably will our lives express, both in prayer and action, the generosity of his saving love.

And that is why it is important to pray for oneself and for others even though it is obviously true that God knows our needs before we ask, and of course we can hardly suppose we are going to change God's will, which is a far better will for everything than we will ever have ourselves when we pray. No, we pray as a proof of that love and will of God; and our prayer helps to make that will effective in a world and in hearts that are uncommonly stubborn and resistant to God. The first place where this can happen is in our own hearts. Our prayer is a sort of continuation by grace and the power of the Holy Spirit of the same will which became incarnate in the person of Jesus Christ for the salvation of all things. That is to say, our prayer of intercession participates in Jesus' own eternal intercession at the right hand of the Father. By it we are led to ask for what God wants to give in answer to prayer.

Intercession also teaches us to pray with faith and hope. What this means is simply that we know we ought to pray for others and we keep on saying we will. But we often seem to have very little expectation that anything will happen because of our prayer. To say we will pray for somebody seems to become little more than a Christian way of wringing our hands. This lack of hope and faith shows, I often think, in the way we so frequently express our petitions. We are always saying, 'if it be your will, grant these prayers . . .', 'answer them in accordance with your will . . .' There is something fishy about the small print. It is as if we do all the talking, saying what we would like, and then, not wanting to have a row with God about it, just say, 'but anything you say, of course!' On the contrary, there ought to be almost an element of protest in our prayer: this ought to be your will; why are things not like this? Intercession includes a struggle.

Of course, we'd be fools to believe we knew God's will for certain. There should always be an element of the provisional in our requests. But we must take responsibility for what we ask in prayer and we must be honest about what we ask. If God were to grant every whim that passed through our hearts, we would be in a mad world: even the fairy story only granted three wishes. But intercession will only grow strong to the extent that we sincerely seek in prayer to understand God's will and to put it into practice ourselves. That calls for faith and hope. It will only grow in so far as we come to share more deeply in the life of Christ and are able to shape our understanding of things according to his will. When Jesus prayed 'if it be according to your will', he was in Gethsemane, fighting to understand things and to see what God was asking of him in those hours of decision. We generally give up a bit earlier on in the struggle.

Compare the story of Jacob wrestling with the angel (Gen. 32.22-30). This is a picture of what it means to persevere in prayer. Jacob would not let go until the angel blessed him. In Jewish terms that is to say until his prayer was answered. Intercession will sometimes include a life-and-death struggle until it is answered; possibly the reason for the struggle is for us to learn God's will and find peace in doing it or accepting it. Jacob was left lame, and prayer can make heavy demands on us; it can leave us powerless, but that can be the way to blessing, too.

In intercession we are seeking the will of God and striving for it in prayer. This means recognizing our own desires for good, as well as surrendering our own selfish preferences that may stand in the way of God's will for a person. That calls for truthfulness, an invincible sense of justice, combined, as God's justice always is, with compassion and mercy. Then we can indeed hope that our prayer will express something of God's love for them. This kind of prayer is, as much as anything, an education in God's love: to intercede for something, especially if it is for someone close to us for whom we pray for a long time, will change us; it will help make us better able to be an answer to prayer for that person, able to minister to them with the love which we have learnt in prayer that God bears to them. Likewise, to pray from the heart for peace will make us more sensitive to our own need for peace, and better peacemakers in our own lives. Intercession is labouring in prayer with the love of God that transforms all things, drawing them to blessing. It is to share in the priesthood and ministry of Christ.

Part of this growing process will include recognition of our poverty in praying for others, of our standing with them in our shared need for God. Another part will be a deep recognition of our communion with them in our humanity and creatureliness. Intercession always goes closely with a deepening of prayer on one's own behalf – to the effect that what we seek for ourselves is intended to help us be an answer to prayer! That is also to take a share of responsibility in praying for others.

Of course, we pray for others in different ways and with different levels of commitment, according to our own relationship to them. This is perfectly natural. A mother will pray for her child more tenderly than for the child next door; there are various degrees of neighbourliness; prayer for our local community will be different from prayer for Queen and country and so on. The various kinds of intercession are a reflection, therefore, of the various kinds of responsibility we have, sometimes an immediate responsibility, sometimes something much less direct: I have an immediate responsibility to ensure justice at home, and a different kind of responsibility to promote justice in our society. Intercession is a vital part of exercising that responsibility. Prayer is almost all I can do for peace in many parts of the world; but if I pray for peace in my family or parish, there's probably quite a lot I should be doing about it, too. How peaceful am I, to begin with? Intercession is never an excuse for inertia; if we strive for God's will in prayer, we should strive for it in our lives. Prayer and life go hand in hand.

It is a mysterious but wonderful privilege, which we have as Christians, not only to express our own desires in prayer, but, far more wonderfully, to express God's desires for our world. An old explanation of the value of intercession is that God wills whatever it may be, but that some things he wills to grant in answer to prayer; he not only wills whatever, but he also wills the prayer that secures his granting it. We will often find it impossible to see what difference our praying makes (except as an expression of concern or wishful thinking), because we have no idea of how a human activity like prayer could possibly make any difference to forces and pressures in the world over which we have absolutely no influence at all ourselves. And yet it is perhaps precisely our concern that God's power should be effective in the world that makes the difference.

We have probably all heard of the extraordinary but unpredictable way in which a butterfly flapping its wings can lead to a tornado which devastates the lives of thousands of people the other side of the world. We are much more aware of the density of forces which govern the behaviour of our planet, let alone the universe. We need not suppose that the world of the Spirit is any less profoundly enmeshed in the circumstances which govern our lives. Teilhard de Chardin once described a picture of a nun praying in a chapel in a desert place, and, as she prays, all the forces of the universe seem to reorganize themselves in keeping with the desires of that tiny praying figure and the axis of the world seems to pass through her desert chapel. In the same vein, there is the Carthusian motto: *stat crux dum volvitur orbis* (the Cross stands firm while the world spins). The power of the intercession and the prayer of monks and nuns, no matter how enclosed or separate from the world, is a vital contribution to the Church's mission in the world. In so far as their enclosure enables them to be more deeply united to Jesus Christ, their prayer is certainly part of the love of his heart for all people. For us to deepen our prayer of intercession, we too have to deepen our own sense of relationship to God in personal prayer. We must always remember that intercession is not about trying to change God's will, but about making it effective in our world.

The Eucharist, the source and summit of prayer

If prayer is inseparable from our being in Christ, prayer becomes part of the way we share in the divine community, which, in this world, is the life of the Church. The Holy Spirit that prays through us changes us by making us part of this new community of Christian life and empowers our efforts to build up the Kingdom of God. This new human reality is the Church: the supreme instance of communal life which is open to the eternal, which expresses the spiritual and helps people engage with it.

For Christians, there is no such thing as private prayer. We should think of prayer, not as private, but as personal prayer; and supremely so in so far as it is made in the person of Christ by those who believe in him. For Christians, all our prayer is part of the life of Christ's Body. We do not lose our identity by being part of Christ's Body. The truth is, rather, that only within this Body do we discover who we really are and become fully personal. Our personal identity is one we find together with all who belong to Christ, and in relation to them. Identity is not a psychological construct (though we do have our *psyches* as well as our physical bodies); it is even more fundamental than that; it lies in our personhood, the way we stand as individuals before God, but united in Christ by the power of the Spirit he has poured out in our hearts.

The Church is the embodiment of that deeper communion, and the sacraments are the means by which it is nourished and sustained. They are the means of salvation, by which we are redeemed and transformed; they spell out our hope of the glory of heaven. What is celebrated thus in the Church's liturgy in public and bodily signs shapes our inward and personal engagement with this reality in prayer. A corollary of this is that the Church's liturgy is the proper environment for Christian prayer: the celebration of the mystery of Christ into whom we have all been baptized. The sacraments, and centrally, of course, the Mass or Eucharist, are the main constituents of this environment. When we pray, then, we are joining our Lord in his work of salvation and transformation. We are entering at a deep and personal level into what we celebrate in the Eucharist, his gift of himself for the salvation of the world, in which he shares with us the food and drink of eternal life.

The Eucharist is the supreme school of prayer. It is so because at its heart is Christ's own prayer to the Father, his offering himself to his Father for the salvation of the whole world. This is the sacrifice that gives meaning to all Christian prayer and, more than that, the Eucharist is the gift to us, shared in Holy Communion, of the food of eternal life. By it we become more and more united to Christ, more and more perfectly his Body, and share more deeply in the life of the Holy Spirit that animates our hearts in prayer, more and more perfectly alive with Christ's life. The Eucharist is the true exercise of priesthood, where the human being of Christ stands before God and on behalf of the world, and where creation finds its source of renewal and grace from the priest's own perfect offering of himself – and we both offer ourselves and are renewed through our communion in him.

The Eucharist is a unique form of prayer because, although many prayers are included in it, it is in the first place an action rather than a prayer, and an action of Jesus Christ rather than ours. But it is a sacramental action, that is, an action that Jesus performs through us, his Body, and an action of the Head through his members. And because we are fully engaged in doing what Jesus does, we use a variety of human signs to express the meaning of what we are engaged in. The complex association of roles different people play, the different signs and gestures that are used, all go towards our being able to say that in what we do at the Eucharist Jesus is offering himself to the Father. That gift once and for all of his own life he made on the Cross, but it continues in the liturgy of the Church through what we do in his name at the altar of the Eucharist.

To pray the Mass, then, means to unite ourselves in the offering Jesus makes of himself to the Father. To draw us into this offering, the parts of the celebration that come first, principally in the Liturgy of the Word, prepare us to share in the Liturgy of the Eucharist. The conclusion of the celebration, rather more briefly but no less significantly, directs us beyond the liturgical celebration to living out the mystery of redemption in the world as people who share in Christ's mission as prophets, priests and kings.

If we follow the celebration through, to start with we find Jesus welcoming us through the person of the priest who celebrates the sacrament. His greeting is in fact made in the name of Jesus himself, 'The Lord be with you'; and the proper response, 'And with your spirit', teaches us that the encounter with Christ that we find in the liturgy is at the level of the Spirit, one in which both priest and people find Christ in each other. This encounter is one with the Risen Lord, and when a bishop celebrates the Eucharist, his words are those Christ used in the Upper Room on Easter Day, 'Peace be with you.'

This initial greeting already does so much to shape the character of the liturgical action as both human and divine in which the priest represents the assembly who are gathered in Christ's name and speaks on their behalf, as in the Collect and other prayers of the celebration, but also represents Christ to them. In a similar way, through the ministry of the readers and singers, people both receive and speak the word of God by which Christ continues to teach his people. But the God who spoke through his prophets finally spoke in the person of the Son, and in the same way the reading of the Gospel is reserved to the deacon or a priest, who is responsible for bringing the message of the Gospel alive for the assembly, who affirm the truth of the Good News of Jesus Christ in the Creed. The first part of the Mass is similar to the Office in that it centres on opening us up to receiving the word of God and responding to it prayerfully in faith and love.

And so the intercession of the Prayer of the Faithful properly passes into the offering of the Eucharist on behalf of the needs of the world. At this point, having found our unity in the fellowship of Christ's word, we use the signs of bread and wine as symbols for the gift of our own lives, the bread of our labour and the wine of our joys and sufferings. These are brought to the priest, who takes them as Jesus did, gives thanks for them, breaks the bread and gives it to us, Jesus' disciples. That is to say, Jesus renews the Last Supper with the stuff of our lives. So Jesus offers himself to the Father through our offering of our lives. But the Last Supper is only a sign of his own offering of himself for our salvation to the Father on the Cross. The breaking and sharing of the bread and the draining of the cup by us is likewise our sharing in Jesus' own offering of his life in the murder of the Cross – but it becomes not a life destroyed but a life given: to the Father for our salvation, and also to us, as sacrificial food, the gift of new and divine life. This life is life through and beyond death, the new life of the Resurrection, life in the Spirit, which God shares with us in Holy Communion.

The heart of the liturgy is the celebration of the mystery of Christ, the Passover of his death and Resurrection above all. The paschal shape of Jesus' human life is also the shape of our life of faith and prayer. We are baptized into our Lord's death; the mysteries of his life must be fulfilled in us. That is how we grow to our full stature in him. In Christian life growth is by dying, not just by expansion or through bits added on. It is a matter of rebirth. The great Carmelite saints, like St Teresa of Avila and St John of the Cross, who have described the higher, mystical reaches of the spiritual life are describing such a pattern of dereliction, death and resurrection to glory as the shape of Christian perfection. But I think we all have to live through such patterns, on a smaller scale and in many and fragmentary ways on the journey of faith.

A precious moment before Holy Communion, which is still part of the Roman Catholic rite of the Eucharist, is the Sign of Peace. Before we are united to our Lord in Holy Communion, we are united with each other in the prayer he taught us, and acknowledge our need for protection against the power of evil, as well as for forgiveness and peace even as we look forward to the establishment of his Kingdom: the peace that Jesus promised at the Last Supper is one that we share in the light and glory of the Resurrection, but it is one that we share because we are conscious of our sins and betrayals of our Lord, as the disciples were when Jesus came among them and said 'Peace be to you.' It is nonetheless a peace we share and minister to each other, and in virtue of which Christ feeds is with his body and blood: 'Lord, I am not worthy to receive you, but only say the word and I shall be healed.' It is a perfect way in which our sharing in the priesthood of Christ is balanced with our acknowledging our need for the fruits of the sacrifice in which we share.

In so many ways the Eucharist expresses the various aspects of our whole life of prayer. At one level it acknowledges our need, our utter dependence on God and our reaching out to him for forgiveness and grace, but more profoundly it is a means by which God continues to work out for the salvation of the world the mystery of Christ. This is the extraordinary privilege of prayer, its glory and joy.

Bibliography

Cloud of Unknowing and other Works (A. C. Spearing, trans., 2001). London: Penguin Classics.

Abhishiktananda (2006), *Prayer*. Norwich: Canterbury Press.

An Interrupted Life: The Diaries and Letters of Etty Hillesum 1941–43, quoted in *Peacemaking Day by Day*. London: Pax Christi 1990.

Augustine of Hippo, *Confessions (Works of Saint Augustine: A Translation for the 21st Century)* (M. Boulding, trans., 2001). New York: New City Press (pocket edition).

Baker, A., *Holy Wisdom* (G. Sitwell, ed., 1972). Wheathampstead: A. Clark Books.

Boase, L. S. (1987), *The Prayer of Faith*. Chicago: Loyola Press.

Butler, B. C. (1983), *Prayer, an Adventure in Living*. London: Catholic Truth Society.

A Carthusian (2006), *Interior Prayer*. Leominster: Gracewing.

A Carthusian (2006), *The Prayer of Love and Silence*. Leominster: Gracewing.

A Carthusian (2006), *They Speak by Silences*. Leominster: Gracewing.

Casey, M. (1991), *Towards God: The Western Tradition of Contemplation*. London: HarperCollins.

Chapman, J., *Spiritual Letters* (R. Hudleston, ed., 2003 with an Introduction by S. Moore). London: Continuum.

De Mello, A. (1984), *Sadhana: A Way to God. Christian Exercises in Eastern Form*. New York: Bantam Doubleday Dell; Reprint edition.

Foster, D. (1999, ed.), *Downside Prayerbook*. London: Burns & Oates.

151

Bibliography

— (2005), *Reading with God: Lectio Divina*. London: Continuum.

Hilton, W. (1991), *Scale of Perfection* (Classics of Western Spirituality; J. Doward Clark and R. Dorward, trans.). New York: Paulist Press.

Hughes, G. (1996), *God of Surprises*. London: Darton, Longman and Todd.

Igumen Khariton of Valamo (1997, ed.), *The Art of Prayer: An Orthodox Anthology* (E. Kadloubovsky and E. M. Palmer, trans., with an Introduction by Kallistos Ware). London: Faber & Faber.

Julian of Norwich, *Revelations of Divine Love* (E. Spearing, trans. 1998, with an Introduction by A. C. Spearing). London: Penguin Classics.

Louf, A. (1974), *Teach us to Pray*. London: Darton, Longman and Todd.

McCabe, H. (1987), 'Prayer', in *God Matters*. London: Geoffrey Chapman. Chapter 18, pp. 215–25.

Merton, T. (1973), *Contemplative Prayer*. London: Darton, Longman and Todd.

Pennington, B. (1982), *Centering Prayer: Renewing an Ancient Christian Prayer Form*. New York: Bantam, Doubleday Dell Publishing Group, Reprint edition.

— (1998), *Lectio Divina: Renewing the Ancient Practice of Praying the Scriptures*. New York: Crossroad Publishing.

St Theophan the Recluse (1992), *The Path of Prayer: Four Sermons on Prayer*. Newbury, MA: Praxis Institute.

Ulanov, A. and Ulanov, B. (1985/2007), *Primary Speech: A Psychology of Prayer*. London: SCM / Westminster: John Knox Press.

Williams, R. (1992), 'Patience with the windings of the soul', *Church Times* 10 January 1992, excerpted from a chapter in J. John (1992, ed.), *Living Tradition: Affirming Catholicism in the Anglican Church*. London: Darton, Longman and Todd.